To Diane,
my old high school chum & life long friend,
Best Wishes,
Janet

Surrounded by ghosts

About the Author

Janet Larkin (Maine) had two near-death experiences before her first encounter with a ghost at age eight. It would be the first of many remarkable experiences that would lead her to experiment with the unknown, and to develop interest in scientific and metaphysical models of larger reality. Drawn to study the mysterious human experience, she went into anthropology where she received her doctorate. In *Surrounded by Ghosts*, she shares the encounters that have helped shape her life.

To Write to the Author

If you wish to contact the author or would like more information about this book, please write to the author in care of Llewellyn Worldwide, and we will forward your request. Both the author and publisher appreciate hearing from you and learning of your enjoyment of this book and how it has helped you. Llewellyn Worldwide cannot guarantee that every letter written to the author can be answered, but all will be forwarded. Please write to:

Janet Larkin
℅ Llewellyn Worldwide
2143 Wooddale Drive
Woodbury, MN 55125-2989

Please enclose a self-addressed stamped envelope for reply, or $1.00 to cover costs. If outside the USA, enclose an international postal reply coupon.

Tales of Pogey Point and Places from my Past

Surrounded by ghosts

JANET LARKIN

Llewellyn Publications
Woodbury, Minnesota

FIRST EDITION
First Printing, 2013

Book design by Bob Gaul
Cover art: House © Steven Puetzer/Photographer's Choice/Getty Images
Shadow life © iStockphoto.com/Volkan Kurt
Cover design by Adrienne Zimiga

Library of Congress Cataloging-in-Publication Data (Pending)
978-0-7387-3598-6

Llewellyn Publications
A Division of Llewellyn Worldwide Ltd.
2143 Wooddale Drive
Woodbury, MN 55125-2989
www.llewellyn.com

Printed in the United States of America

Contents

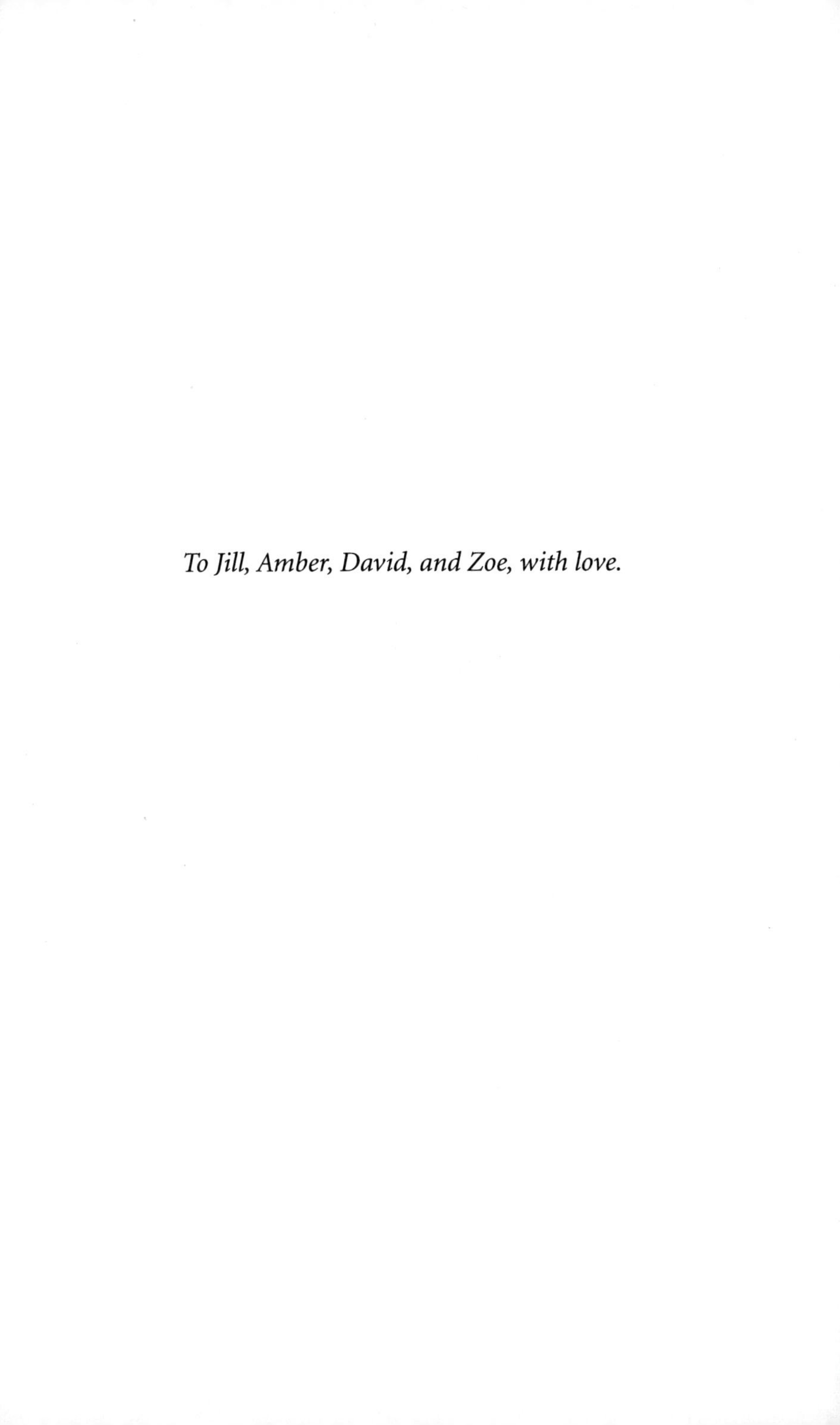

To Jill, Amber, David, and Zoe, with love.

Introduction

It was a Sunday morning in France and the sun was up over the hilly terrain of Champagne. Amber, my fifteen-year-old daughter and traveling companion, was sharing cheese and a baguette with me for breakfast as we traveled the northern French countryside in our compact rental car. It was our last day of our first European adventure. Vineyards stretched over the valleys and hillsides in all directions and the impeccably neat vines reminded me of cornrowed hair. Each estate was blessed with gigantic crucifixes. Jesus was everywhere.

We approached a hill heading into a village. There was something in the road up ahead, a girl on a bike, it turned out. I slowed down, expecting she'd move to the side, but she held a course straight down the middle. *Maybe it's the way around here*, I thought. I heard church bells ringing.

People were walking alongside the road toward the church. I eased off the gas and shifted into second, hearing the engine struggle with gravity. We were just creeping along and I was getting a little annoyed because we had a lot of territory to cover. We had a six-thirty flight from DeGaulle and most of the way back was interstate, but we needed to allow for time to return the car and for the two-hour check-in.

It was Amber who, less concerned with time, noticed the biker's peculiarity. We could only see her back, but from her size she looked to be about twelve. She was very thin; her legs were skinny. Her hair hung freely, her crown sported a gigantic bow that matched the one tied at the back of her print dress. She wore knee socks. It was not modern dress; it looked vintage. The bike was an old model, too, the kind with fenders.

I glanced at the people walking along the road for comparison, to see if old-fashioned dress was the norm here. They all look fairly normal to me, except none of them were smiling—as though the church bells were summoning them against their will. They cast looks of irritation back at us, as if we were committing sacrilege by traveling on the Sabbath. It made me wonder if this road was closed on Sunday. I'd become aware that there was no other traffic. I wondered if they could tell we were Americans; we didn't feel very welcome in Paris. Amber had had enough of this attitude and, monitoring the passenger-side window, she said they were all creeps.

After several minutes the land flattened out and we arrived at the village where the road broadened. The girl on the bike had room to scoot aside now, but she was stubborn; it was like she wanted us to follow her to church. I moved out around her and when we passed, she turned her head. "*What the hell*?" Amber muttered. "Mom, did you see that?"

I had, and I was just as shocked as she was to learn that this twelve-year-old girl in knee socks and bows was a frail old woman. Her chest and stomach were nearly concave. Her face was rowed like the vineyards—and I thought a lifetime of picking grapes in the sun was what put them there. I was startled enough to look twice, to check to see if it was a mask an adolescent might find amusing.

"Oh. My. God!" Amber laughed, delighted by surprise. "What was *that*?" She went for her camera, hoping to get a head-on view out the back window.

I tried to be practical. Rural French people lived very long lives. Amber said "Even so, riding a bike up a steep grade at a hundred isn't normal, there's something wrong about it. Wrong about this town. The people act like zombies." She wanted to stop and get the old woman's picture. She knew no one would believe us. I told her it would be offensive, that we had no time. Anyway, the woman was gone now. She'd disappeared from my rearview mirror. I reasoned she was lost in the crowd, though I knew the human trickle was too thin to have absorbed her and the bike.

I was left with that sense of wonder one gets when trying to gauge the incredible. Amber was zooming, panning the steps with her camera, the other side of the village street. Frustrated, she turned forward as we left behind a little French village we'd never again find on the map.

How the Ghosts Got into Jars

A big part of my life has been trying to gauge the incredible, that feeling that raises the suspicion that not everything is as it should be. You're going along just fine one minute and the next you're aware you've just passed beyond this time zone, you've slipped into some outer limit, it hits you in the gut and digests slowly. Whoever the surprising old woman was, Amber and I both had that feeling that *something had just happened.*

Neither Amber nor I had verbalized it for several miles, until we'd gained a safe distance and had the time to put what we saw and how we felt together, but, *hadn't we just seen a ghost*? I remember that split second when our eyes met with that question. The incongruities couldn't really be normalized, whether it was the old woman's unusual attire or her athletic ability, it jarred us. These kinds of jarring experiences are what this book is about. It's written without exaggeration by an ordinary woman, a girl who grew up on a northern Utah fruit farm, married young, had two kids, got divorced, became an anthropologist, then spent her life teaching. Nothing about me is extraordinary, except that in between the kids and career, there were a few ghosts.

I saw my first one at eight. It was my grandmother, and not really knowing what to do with her I put the experience away. An eight-year-old craves the ordinary. I could have chosen a box or any other metaphoric container to store Grandma in, but her visit occurred in the fall and coincided with canning season. Mom and I were in the middle of bottling peaches. This event in our home was more than practical tradition, it was autumn ritual—good for the soul as is any activity shared in a kitchen with mothers, and good nourishment for the body.

More importantly for me at that age, the jars were things of beauty. After they'd been processed and placed on towels lining the cabinets to cool, we had works of art on our kitchen counters. Colors fresh from the tree—like the ruby-ness of pie cherries, or the faint yellow of pears shining through clear syrup in glistening jars topped with bright golden crowns—were nothing less than glorious. I used to think that if we took them to the state fair, the blue ribbon would be given to the deep vivid flesh of the famous Utah peach.

This activity was soulful for me, and Grandma had been no stranger to a jam or pickle jar; I guess Ball jars came more naturally to both of us for holding soulful things. I'd already rendered many a quart bottle useful for capturing elusive creatures, mostly winged momentary treasures like June bugs or boxelder bugs, an occasional butterfly, or the more terrestrial crickets and grasshoppers. The whole purpose was to get a closer look, slow it down long enough to understand it, which for me involved coming eye to eye with the bug. Once I had a pretty good notion of it, I'd set it free.

The essence of what I'm doing here is what I did with the bugs, coming eye to eye with experience that has long been sequestered and left unexamined to the extent it deserved. To the extent I had any real notion of it, and that's a shame because I have probably had more ghosts than I ever did bugs. I didn't mean for it to become habit; at eight I had no way of knowing that other jars would follow, that my next fifty years would be punctuated with enough demons, angels, and synchronicity to provide me a bottle collection I'd one day shine up and tell the world about.

The ghost jar metaphor is useful on many levels. Imagine a string of empty, dust- and cobweb-covered bottles jumbled together on a cool, dark fruit-room shelf. These jars only appear to be empty because they contain experience, something that can't be seen any better than ghosts. It's a useful way for conveying how I compartmentalized the spiritual experience—putting the fruit of it up for a less busy day; and placing the jars in the dark signifies the way we often shove experience that disrupts ordinary thinking to the back of the mind. I guess the jars signify the course of least resistance.

The location is also significant to me. My mother's fruit room always had a cobweb or two. I hated being sent down to the basement to retrieve a bottle of peaches or pie cherries; I could smell the dankness before getting there and this place was pitch dark, surrounded on three sides by foundation like a walk-in grave. I could be surrounded by ghosts on all four sides if I went in, so I tried reaching for the jars from the threshold. I sometimes scared myself, pretending Dracula might be in there, way to the back in one of the unlit earthen corners.

If I wanted light I worked for it. A single bulb dangled overhead and I had to fish around in the dark for the invisible string that pulled it on. I tried taking the scare out of it by turning it into an amusement, experimenting to see how intuitive I was at locating the string with my eyes closed. Instead of flailing around for it I'd stand at the threshold and contemplate the string, see it in my mind's eye, and at this I grew pretty successful; I could often reach out and touch it immediately. Later, as an added feature, I tried testing the speed of my ability, seeing if I could yank on the light before Dracula or some equivalent bit. I always did. I really did wonder what, besides cobwebs, my hand sweeping the blackness might find; it was a small enclosed space where the light never reached completely to the back of the shelves where something could have been hiding.

A place such as that seemed a fit one for stashing ghosts.

The reason I'm telling the stories of the ghosts now is because it wasn't until now that I could tell them completely, as honestly, as they deserved. Up to now I've examined jars but left parts of them in the dark—those emotional details and secret impressions sometimes left out of the telling because they're too personal to let go. It results in only half a story, one that's filled with verbs like the one above, boiled down to what we saw and what happened. In this book I plan to go beyond description because the intuitions and spiritual depth of the experience make these ghosts real. That wondrous sense of the incredible is stored in images and emotions that your body doesn't forget, emotions that arise from instinct meant to detect the unseen and discern its nature, though it's usually this part that's left out of the telling because it's too dear to share with skeptical family and friends who'll just look at you funny. At fifty-six one still craves ordinary, more or less. Still, it's these details that prove the case. The spiritual details are necesary to understand a spiritual case.

Take that girl on the bike.

When slowing the story down to each remembered impression, it goes like this: she was too far away to make out clearly when I first noticed her, all I knew was that there was something up ahead that I should pay attention to. I immediately tensed up because I remember thinking *it shouldn't be there.* Some instinct had been triggered. I became increasingly anxious as we neared the back of her and were forced to slow down. I didn't know why I felt so uncomfortable, so I transformed the feeling into fretting about getting to the airport on time; it seemed like something I could handle. But that wasn't really it. I was uncomfortable because I was feeling confused about why I would suddenly feel this way on approaching this obscure village. To me it looked like any other, yet my antennae were up.

We followed the girl a few minutes until I realized she wasn't budging. For a second I wondered if she was claiming the road as some sort of local right. That was when uncomfortable turned into troubling. I couldn't decide what I was dealing with—there was too much ambiguity in the situation. Earlier, Amber had warned me to "watch out for that girl on the bike," thinking I might not see her, but I had and was already sensing it wasn't a kid. I just couldn't figure out who else would have the strength to pedal up that grade the way she did; she seemed to float up it, taking long, uncontrolled strokes that almost made her look like she was adrift.

Well, that was just silly.

In trying to figure it out I looked for indication of age. Her flowing long hair was brown, indicating she was young rather than old, though the dress indicated old-fashioned taste. I transformed this confusion into a strategy for trying to get past her. The idea that she might be a ghost never entered my head; it's not a conclusion I am quick to jump to. Even when we did get a closer look, my rational mind was still trying to sort it out. We were startled at her age and condition, but I didn't immediately attribute it to her being unworldly.

What made me go there was her expression. More or less coming "eye to eye with the bug."

Her nearly inimical glance was so unexpected that it quite literally took my breath away. It wasn't the kind expected from strangers—they may give indifference or a frown, but not generally the Evil Eye. But what reason would she have had to curse us? What was behind the sour intent? Reason couldn't sort it out so instinct moved in, informing me this *wasn't normal,* something out of the ordinary was happening. There'd been a physical shift in consciousness. Although we were both moving, time seemed to slow down for that jarring moment where we discovered her true identity. In that fraction of time, we occupied one space that was neither solely hers nor solely ours and we were equally aware of it as an intrusion. It was that split-second recognition that made the cellular impression stick.

I didn't actually just lose sight of her, but Amber did when she went fussing with her camera. My eyes were glued to the rearview mirror because I needed to verify my impressions, I slowed down to a crawl so that Amber could shoot her pictures but also to give me that opportunity. The biker hadn't gotten lost among the churchgoers—that was just the most logical conclusion to draw, a less silly thing to say than what I saw. She had actually turned into a brick alley just after we'd passed. It surprised me because the church was on the opposite side of the street and I'd thought she was headed there. As she parted ways with the others I remember thinking, "She isn't one of them, she's not part of the community." I got the idea she was a pariah, the village outcast, only later understanding it meant "dead."

The reason I don't generally include that detail in the story—just skip to where it dawned on us later down the road that we'd just run into a ghost—is because I saw her do a very ghostly thing then. It's a memory I usually hold close to the chest for fear of sounding absurd or like I'm resorting to cliché, but the old woman masquerading as a child literally vanished, faded out before she even got around the bricked corner of that building. It was a deliberate spectacle, I felt, because it was so obvious; almost as if she was hoping her disappearing act would upset me.

But I'd already passed being upset. Seeing her vanish right before my eyes in my rearview mirror left me in a state of wonder.

One

How It Might Have Gotten Started

Day one of life and death was already breathing down my neck.

I don't know if there is cosmic significance to one's birth date, but I was born exactly forty-six years before September 11th became a day of infamy, for forty-six years it was an unblemished and, for me, personally special day. Though back in 1954, September 11th held no particular national significance. Similar threats to those in 2001 were afoot in a northern Utah town: Brigham City's hospital nursery was also under an airborne attack, this one by whooping cough bacteria, that soon after birth began terrorizing my eight-pound, two-ounce, otherwise robust body.

Back then whooping cough was deadly for an infant—and apparently I died.

Mom would tell me how I lived the first few months of life in an oxygen tent struggling to breathe, and how I came home from the hospital with my survival in doubt. "They told me you'd either make it or you wouldn't," Mother said. "Isn't that just something? Telling a mother that. I was upset at old Doc Felt for a long time after."

She sat vigil at the oxygen tent over the bassinette at her bedside, tortured by the whoop-whoop of the cough stressing tiny lungs, listening for my breathing, on guard for the moment it stopped—a new mother with four other kids, exhausting herself. But it paid off. She was there to sound the alarm when it finally happened, rousing my father and "pertineer half the neighborhood" to do something about her dying baby girl. My mother was a superhero.

From here my father usually told the story. From here he got to be the superhero. He called my uncles to come over to the house and help him give me a father's blessing. "You were just a pink little thing in a white nightgown," he'd begin reliving the experience. My dad was a freckled Irishman who loved telling stories, and I liked hearing them, especially if they were about me.

Dad's two oldest brothers lived on farms like ours across the highway. Dad told me how Rulon and Uncle Curly assisted him, how they made a cradle with their rough old farmer's hands to hold me in the circle they'd made, kneeling and bowing their heads to God in the living room.

Mother and Uncle Curly's wife, Aunt Naomi, stood near, praying with them. "I could feel you struggling to breathe, Jinnit Girl," Dad told me. "I knew we were losing you."

I have no explanation for why he always called me that, he just did. I'd say, "Dad, my name's *Janet. Janet Sue*," and he'd chuckle, "I know, Jinnit Girl."

"You were being tortured by those bugs," he continued. "Running a temperature you couldn't fight off. Couldn't sleep with all the coughing, your little lungs had had enough." He shook his head remembering. "I felt it when you gave up—you went limp as a ragdoll. No life a-tall to you. All of us in that room felt the soul slip out of your body." Dad paused. I thought he was suppressing a sniffle, but he was lighting a cigarette.

"So what did you do?!?" I asked, wanting to hear about the miracle.

"Well," he winked. "I prayed harder."

He said he understood that he had to fight for my right to live. That he couldn't let it happen to my mother. That he made a bargain.

The reason I mention this is because many folks who've had near-death experiences claim a heightened spiritual existence and enhanced psychic awareness. My experience would certainly qualify as a near death. As I keep searching my soul for answers my head says it's possible, that infant trauma could stimulate the development of a sixth sense.

Another trauma worth mentioning occurred when I was a toddler.

I grew up in the Wasatch basin of the Rocky Mountains on a twenty-four-acre apple farm. There were peaches, apricots, cherries, and pears, but mostly we grew apples. I was born into a Mormon family of six kids. Kay and Dale were already teenagers by the time I happened, and Judy and Kent were pre-adolescents. My brother Rodney was born a year later, making us the babies of the family. As Mom had her hands full with kids, a home, and the orchards, my big sister Judy tended to me a lot.

There were more chores to do on the farm than just babysitting, and the story goes that one day Mother needed the garbage hauled down to the burn area. Dale and Kent just kept putting it off so Judy volunteered to help out. She said she was trying to unhook the furrowing disk so she could hook up the trailer, when I came running through the field aiming to hitch a ride. I apparently threw a tantrum when she told me no, so she put me up next to the wheel hub to stop my hollering. She said she knew Mother would have a fit, but she guessed it was better than running me over.

As it turned out, she wasn't that familiar with the tractor. She jerked the gears trying to find reverse and I went tumbling. It just so happened that when she became aware of what had happened and stopped the vehicle, its back tire halted directly on the side of my head—the circular blades of the disk just feet away. Then, with the ultimate skill and quick thinking she brags about having at fourteen, she told how she very carefully backed off me, dreading the whole time to hear the crunch of a three-year-old's skull. She laughs when she tells me there were actually tire treads up the side of my face. It's safe to laugh about it now.

She jumped down and swooped me up, running through the orchards to Mother. "Janet's dead!" she screamed to the back of the house, and Mom came down the dirt road and retrieved me. This required a visit to old Doc Felt who said I was a remarkable child. He was surprised my skull wasn't squashed or that my neck wasn't broken. He probably thought of calling social services. He sent us home without even an X-ray and thought all of my hollering was because I was just scared. He winked at Mom and told her the same thing he'd told her three years earlier, that I'd either make it or not.

Fortunately for me and for Judy, both the ground that time of year and the bones in my head were soft, because Dad wasn't around this time to give me his blessing. I don't know what sort of bargain Dad had made with God, but it wasn't sticking around and raising me. He'd left his general contracting business to drive a truck right around the time this happened. I've wondered if this heightened intuition that's allowed me a relationship with spirit has to do with him. They say Celtic souls are sensitive, and his side of the family originated in Ireland as O'Larkins from County Galway.

One spring I visited Ireland with Judy and my oldest daughter Jill. We loved it; each county has its own authentic charm, but all of us felt a deeply personal kinship with Connemara. We're usually a pretty talkative bunch, but as

I drove alongside the dreary peat bogs that stretched to the barren spines of the Twelve Bens—haunting mountains when seen through mists sweeping the moors—a quiet came over the car. The hush came from knowing that we *could* be rooted in this austere landscape, that ours was the type of family to have risen from a place where the very bedrock poked through the ground. It wasn't farming country, what we were used to, but to the soul it felt familiar.

I don't know how much ancestry plays a part in one's spirituality or psychic sensibility, but it's just as likely that early physical trauma or an early near-death experience is responsible. All I know is that with this sensitivity came the ability to perceive ghosts.

Two

Grandma's Visit

After Mom and Dad's divorce, I got a new babysitter. Mother had to leave farming to pay the mortgage, and after some technical training, she got a job working night shifts at Sperry Rand soldering electrical components. By this time Judy was married and gone, so Kent got the chore of babysitting Rod and me. He wasn't into it. He was a teenager with a fancy car, which was why Rod and I were home alone on that cool fall night when I was eight and awoke troubled.

I knew something had woke me but I couldn't figure out what. It had begun to rain, and I wondered if that was it; here and there a drop was striking the windowpane. Or maybe the phone had rung—or the doorbell. Oh, I very much hoped it wasn't the doorbell; it was midnight and all the lights were off, nobody up to any good would be out this time of night in stormy weather. Just Kent.

I couldn't decide what it was so I decided not to care, I just got up and headed down the hall toward Mother's room. I must have been sleepwalking, only dreaming that I was awake, because somehow I walked down the hall and ended up in Willard cemetery. Willard cemetery was where all of our family and everyone we knew were laid to rest. It was situated on a hilly piece of ground on the western bench of the Wasatch Rockies. From there we could look down over orchards and past alfalfa fields to Willard Bay—a sort of extension of the Great Salt Lake. Looking the other way was Willard Peak, a massive wall of vertical rock that in the springtime services a temporary waterfall.

I guess I was standing at my grandparents' graves because I looked down through the ground and saw them both lying in their caskets. I thought, *How did I get here? Wow, I musta flew.* Then, *why am I here? If I can fly why didn't I go somewhere better, like Africa?* I never knew either of my grandparents. Thinking about them was a new idea to me.

I was suddenly overwhelmed with emotion. It was the saddest feeling I'd known in my young life—I'm not sure I've felt anything so extreme since—my ribs actually ached from the sadness of my grandparents being there. I was suddenly terribly worried about them. I was cold and wet. I thought that they must have been too. Cold, wet, *and* dead. I was utterly crestfallen.

Something drew me back to Mother's bedroom where I was sitting up and crying, grateful it was a dream because the alarm clock told me Mom wouldn't be home for two more whole hours. But *somebody was* there, something was different from when I crawled out of bed. I didn't think I was alone. I suddenly needed to pee, but I didn't want to go down the hall to the bathroom. I decided to hold it. Then I saw her, a woman was standing between the bed and the dresser, right next to the bedside. She was looking right at me and I was suddenly ashamed of crying. She either didn't approve or she was letting me know there was no need of it. She was a tall, slender woman who seemed to float just above the floor. I wondered how she got into the house and into Mother's room. I had the impression she came in through the ceiling. She had deep, gentle brown eyes and a proud forehead, her dark hair was piled up at the crown, the rest pinned back into a bun. She was wearing a high-necked dress. It wasn't Mother: she wasn't slender and she hadn't come home from work yet.

"Don't be afraid," the lady said to me.

"I'm not," I told her, though neither of us were actually moving our mouths; we were just thinking at each other.

"I'm your grandmother," she introduced herself, "your mom's mother."

"I know," I said, and I did, I knew it was Grandma Fluhman though we'd never met. I almost thought it was silly her identifying herself. I'd known her forever.

She knew what I'd been dreaming. "I'm not cold," she got right to the point. The messages came in telegraphic spurts. “I’m not wet. I’m not there. I’m okay.” I wondered about Grandpa. “We’re both happy,” she let me know. “Now stop crying,” she said firmer than I was used to being spoken to. “You should know better.” I thought about it. I *did* know better. She softened a little, knowing I was embarrassed, “You’re going to be okay.” I thought the last thing she said before she left was “Don’t worry,” she was going to keep an eye on me. While I understood she’d meant to comfort me, I was left in a state between fear and wonder. Had this really happened? Who was going to believe me? I remember searching the dim room from the safety of the bed to see if there were any more people in it.

I was afraid to tell Mother the next day. Although she was my biggest ally, I didn’t think she’d believe I’d seen Grandma’s ghost; she’d think I was just trying for some attention, maybe bragging or something. My three brothers would surely ridicule me, they were all jokers at my expense. I managed to keep it to myself all morning, but by noon I was ready to burst my britches. I just had to get Mom’s opinion on it. It was Saturday and we were sitting at the kitchen table while she was paying bills. I wasn’t sure how to begin so I just spilled it.

“I saw Grandma Fluhman last night,” I timidly ventured, fearful of a dirty look.

Mother must not have heard, she tore out a check, stuck it in an envelope and licked the flap. She threw it into a pile for mailing and went on to the Utah Power & Light bill.

"I had this dream about Grandpa and Grandma bein' in the Willard cemetery," I told her, committed to having this heard, though playing it safe by staging it in a dream. "I was crying because they were down there in the ground and Grandma came and told me not to worry. She said they aren't in the ground, they're warm and happy."

I thought this should make Mom happy, too, but she was getting irritated. She *ripped* off the next check. I decided I'd better shut up.

Hours passed. We were making supper. Fish sticks and homemade hash browns were frying in the electric skillet. Mother had been quiet all day and I'd taken it to mean she was upset with me. She had her back turned, doing something in the sink. I was waiting at the Formica-top table where there was a big plate glass window that showed off the mountains. There was a view of those mountains everywhere from the front of the house. It was still raining. The window was steaming up.

Mom turned around and wiped her hands on the dish towel slung over her shoulder. I could tell she was getting ready to say something, but she wasn't sure if she should. I knew it was about Grandma because it was she who had been between us all day. I could just hear what my Mom was thinking—my resurrection of the dead was some form of sacrilege. Ordinary folks, especially children, didn't receive visions, just men did—in Utah, it was prophets. Heaven didn't work through little girls. I suddenly felt pretty foolish, like I was a bad kid. I was regretting saying anything because it had upset her and I was embarrassed now. I didn't want to see Grandma ever again.

Things like that probably didn't run through Mother's head, but her quiet hadn't been disapproval with me, it was over a personal disappointment. She said she missed her mother terribly after the divorce, it was hard going it alone without financial or social support. For years no one knew where Dad even was, so he hadn't been of any help—I had a deadbeat dad and she was too proud to rely on the state, or even the church's own welfare program. Instead, she'd gotten work and sold off the farm acre by acre. But it wasn't so easy to fix social damages like divorce in a small, fifties Mormon town. This was a time when single mothers were rare, and we were in a place where single mothers were unheard of; I was the only kid in school whose parents had split, and it somehow made *me* different. But it wasn't as hard on me as it was on Mom, who lost her circle of friends; she quit going to church because of the gossip, and from then on Mom was different too.

She often brought up how hard it'd been to cope when Dad ran off and left her with six kids to raise on a broken heart. She said it wasn't supposed to go like that. She deserved a happy home and the Betty Crocker white picket fences after twenty-five years of trying to make it happen. Why, after all her prayers, had she been ignored in her time of need? She'd made a pact with her mother that if after she died she still lived, she would return to let Mom know. She'd engaged Grandma in private conversations when she was looking for strength, had prayed for the assurance that heaven was there and it was all worth it.

Why hadn't Grandma come to her? They'd had an arrangement. Why had she chosen her granddaughter?

Mom forced a smile and came and sat down at the table across from me, realizing, I guess, that Grandma *had* made good on her promise. "How'd she look?" she asked.

This experience was kept between myself and Mother, safe from sibling ridicule, but for both of us it spurred wonder about ghostly agendas. Why *would* her own mother leave her uncomforted when her solace crumbled? Why, if Grandma were going to expend the energy, would she instead choose to comfort a kid having a bad dream? I remember feeling unworthy of such a marvelous thing and told Mother it might have been a mistake. Maybe Grandma had meant to visit her, I just happened to be in her bed.

Three

The Ghost of a Murdered Mother

By the time I was eleven, somebody else owned our orchards, all twenty-three acres of them. We salvaged the acre our fifties-style yellow brick house stood upon, but Mother had been forced to sell off the property next door to do so. This had been Grandma and Grandpa's place, the house where Mother and my Uncle Dick had been born, where Mom and Dad had lived when they were first married and where the older four kids were born. Letting it go had been heartbreaking to her. The new owner spruced up the old white clapboard, put on a new roof, and turned it into a rental property. Just after I turned twelve, the Ward family moved in. They were private folks like we were. They didn't go to church either. I didn't even know if they were Mormons. They had four sons; the oldest, Donny, had a wild reputation.

One night I was again wakened from sleep, the way I'd been at eight, only this time it was much later than midnight and it was more like I'd been jolted conscious. I sat up and looked about the dim room for what wakened me—I thought it was a sound. Something drew me to my closet where I found my old tap-shoe box had fallen from the shelf above the hangers. It was odd, because it was the only box up there and it was like an antique from when I was six, usually pushed to the corner at the back with a sweater or two in front. I stooped down and picked the box up, put the black patent leather size-four tap shoes back into it, and replaced the lid. Had it really happened? Well, I *was* standing there holding the box…

I placed the box back up on the shelf and returned to bed, but I didn't lie down. I just sat under the covers waiting, feeling like I was *supposed* to be up. I felt that box wanted me awake for some reason, and I had a sinking feeling that whatever was going to happen wasn't going to be good. Mother wasn't home or I'd have gone and told her. By this time Kent was in Vietnam, so now I was the babysitter. After a few minutes of nothing else happening, I figured the creepy feeling I had was simply because I'd been dreaming something creepy. The shoe box? Well, maybe we had a mouse.

Then I heard a thud. I perked back up because I was sure it had something to do with why I was awake. Then I heard two more of these thuds, maybe more—I'd stopped counting. I was trying to figure out what the heck it was. They seemed to originate somewhere outside to the left of me, which would have meant they were coming from our garage or the Wards' on the other side of it. I heard the echo diffuse above the orchards to the west. Another thud. Nothing was registering. I realized I'd never heard these sounds before. The shoe box hadn't left the shelf; I'd been keeping an eye on it because I felt it might fall again any minute. Then the disturbing punctuations ceased. I waited a minute or two to make sure, then passed it off as having no importance to me. Since I had school the next day my first thought was to go back to sleep. But I couldn't. The weird sounds had quit, but I had the feeling it wasn't the end of things. I thought I ought to get up and check out the rest of the house; I was in charge now.

I got up and turned on my overhead bedroom light, then checked out the closet again anyway. It was stupid to blame a mouse for a flying box; tap shoes were heavier than ordinary shoes, so unless we had a rat, that box couldn't have budged out from behind the sweaters. And we didn't have rats—I'd never seen one in my life. But boxes didn't have intentions either. I couldn't shake the notion that *someone* had used it to get my attention. Naturally, my first thought was of Grandma. "Was that you?" I whispered into the closet, certain that the "you" would be understood. I got no answer, but I suddenly got the notion to go into the kitchen.

I went and checked the locks on both the front and back doors, then turned on the kitchen light above the sink. When I'd done the dishes earlier I'd overstacked the drying tray, leaving pots and pans to sort of teeter totter on top of each other. I wondered if they'd fallen and could explain the thuds; a stainless steel frying pan might have made that sound if it dropped on kitchen carpeting. But as far as I could tell, nothing in the kitchen had moved an inch. I was standing at the porcelain sink wedged into a corner where there was a panoramic view of our big yard, the double driveway, and the Wards' next door. I noticed there was a light on at their house and it surprised me because they weren't usually up that late.

I gave the yard a good looking over, not knowing what I was looking for; I guess anything to explain the uneasy feeling I had that I was waiting for something bad. It felt like something bad had taken hold of the night. My first fear was for Mom; she had to make that seventy-mile drive back from Salt Lake all alone in the dark after eight hours of soldering tiny electrical parts. She was always complaining how night driving tired out her eyes after eight hours of looking into a magnifying glass. I prayed off the dread of a call from the police. I told God I was too young to lose my mother, I had just turned twelve and I didn't have a dad, so would he please protect her and our black Chevy. Protect me from being an orphan. I added my perpetual concern about Mother's age; she'd been forty when she'd had me, she wasn't young like the other kids' moms, and at twelve it seemed to me that fifty-two was around the time people started dropping.

I stood at the sink almost instinctively waiting, trying to sort out this weirdness. Maybe it wasn't anything worse than the residue of a bad dream. Maybe the electricity in the air meant Mom would get home early tonight. What was up with that tap box, though?

Then, out of the dead of the night, sirens came screaming down Highway 89. Four Utah state patrol cars passed through our small rural town and straight to the Wards' driveway. I figured it had to do with Donny, the one with the reputation, but it was strange that they'd need so many cops to arrest one guy. I ran and told Rod to come quick, something was happening next door. The two of us watched as the sheriff got out a megaphone and began shouting for Donny to come out of the house. It was cool, like in the movies. Then the cop called out for Donny's dad, Mr. Ward. Then for Mrs. Ward. We waited, they waited, but nobody came out.

The police moved in then, and a few minutes later the ambulances arrived. It was all over. I told Rod I bet we'd see some dead bodies coming out of Grandpa and Grandma's old house, at least we'd have a good story to tell Mom when she got back. Then I saw a policeman crossing over into our yard and select the cement walk leading to the front door.

We always used the one that was under the breezeway that connected the garage to the house. Before I could think of what a policeman could want, he rang the front doorbell—the door only strangers used.

I turned on the porch light and opened it up to two people, the cop and a woman who I assumed was a plain-clothed police woman. I remember telling them my mom wasn't at home, but the cop still asked if he could come in. He was holding a baby, so I let him. The woman followed him into the foyer but soon left us, I had the notion she'd gone into the kitchen and I was wondering what right she had to come in and snoop around. I wondered if we were in trouble. When she never rejoined us, I reasoned she must have gone back over to the Wards'.

The highway patrolman told me that some people had been shot next door and one of them was this baby's mother. She was dead, and so was the baby's father. The kid was about three months old and I could see blood on her pajamas. He said they were waiting for a relative to come get her but it might take an hour or two; they were coming from a ways away. He'd seen the kitchen light on and thought we might take her in until they got there. It'd sure be a help; they had their hands full over at the Ward house, not enough help to watch the child, they'd have to wait until somebody from Weber County responded and that'd tie things up.

I didn't remember saying yes before he ditched her with me and gave me her bottle, but I noticed it was only half-full and was already wondering what to do if it didn't last a couple of hours. I was wondering if the kid came with diapers. Out of the blue there I was, standing in the miracle living room in the same dead of night where twelve years earlier Dad had held another infant, and prayed for her.

Rod went back to bed, leaving me to tend to the girl myself. I didn't know the baby's name, the cop hadn't said, but I held her as she slept and thought about the situation. How just an hour ago all was well with the world and now here I was holding a brand-new orphan. How her mother'd just become a ghost. I wondered whether I'd mistaken the mother for the police woman simply because she was there with the cop when I had opened the door. I was sure she'd followed him in but hadn't left, so I went and checked out the kitchen. It was something. Maybe it was because I was twelve and had some experience, or because the mother was such a fresh ghost, but I could virtually see her; her presence was so there and the air was thick.

I don't think my physical eyes saw her, but some inner sight did because I knew details about her. She was a petite person; at twelve I was taller. She was shook up and standing in the corner next to the cupboard where we put the phone, apologizing for being there but letting me know she was going to be staying for a brief time. My impressions had been right! She hadn't been with the cop, but with the baby. I told her I knew she was there and that it was okay, and after that she seemed to relax—not because I gave her permission but because we could communicate.

She followed the baby and me back into the living room, where she stood in front of the plate glass window with the dark clear night and stars shining over the mountains as backdrop. From there she watched us the rest of the night. Over the hours I got to know my ghostly companion. I imagined her a scared young woman not much more than a teenager, and I had the feeling someone else was with her; several who were assisting her but holding back from me. I picked up on her emotions the best. I felt her concern about what had just happened, and knew she was initially troubled because she didn't know who I was or if she could trust me with her child. I told her not to worry, I babysat all my nieces and nephews—I had eleven of them—and then how sorry I was that she'd died. Perhaps my own fears were playing into things, but I suddenly felt the pain of a mother and child divided. I felt this young woman's disappointment in not being there to raise her little girl, and then an immense sadness swept over me for the child. I imagined years ahead to the day she'd learn how her parents died, and I felt her mother's remorse and anguish in apprehending that day.

For a twelve-year-old whose private fears had physically manifested, it was an intense sorrow to experience even vicariously, nearly as intense as the sorrow I'd felt seeing my grandparents in the grave. I instinctively defaulted to

Grandmother's advice and told the girl not to worry. I was aware of how crazy it seemed for a human to give a ghost spiritual assurance.

Then I said a prayer to at least make myself feel better.

Mom got back from work way before the relatives came to pick the baby up. It was almost eight in the morning by the time they did. By then we'd learned the story about how a Brigham City cop had shot up the whole family. Donny and this guy's wife had been having an affair and had finally decided to take it to the next level; she'd just asked her cop husband for a divorce so she and Donny could start a life together. That night the cop got drunk after his shift and drove down to Willard to settle the score. The first shot killed Donny, the second, the cop's own wife. I found out that she'd been in the kitchen holding the baby at the time, and the child had fallen with her mother to the floor. It accounted for the bloody pajamas. Mr. Ward, who'd tried stepping in, was an unfortunate, unintended, nonfatal casualty before the shooter turned the gun on himself.

The thuds that echoed over our peaceful orchards had been bullets.

Nothing like this happened out in our part of Willard, technically South Willard, the outskirts of a small Mormon town. It afforded me a small amount of celebrity to have it happen right next door. My friends were eager to hear the story of how I heard the gunshots and how the baby had arrived. It alone was a good enough story that I could leave out the tap-shoe box that preceded things and how I was sure someone had wanted me awake and available. I never mentioned how the spirit in the closet had gotten me up to turn on the kitchen light so the child had a safe place to be, or how the ghost came and went with the baby.

For the part where boxes flew off shelves by themselves, I'd need another jar.

Four

The Bogey Man

My next encounter with the otherworldly took place when I was seventeen. Of all the experiences I've had with beings beyond the veil, this is the only one I'd like to keep in its jar. I'd like to deny it any space in my memory because this jar's unsettling, a red herring in my overall philosophy of things. It rubs against my grain because I don't want to believe in demons; I wasn't raised to believe in them. Demons are metaphors. Still, I think what I describe comes close to one.

My teenage years were unextraordinary in every way. Although I'd seen Grandma's ghost, and empathized with the murdered mother's, the experiences slipped into the rest of my life without much notice. The only halfway unusual experience I had was at a slumber party when we got out a Ouija board. I don't know who brought the board, but we used it in our front room—the same one I came back to life in. With Mother working nights I could get away with it, but she'd have killed me if she'd known. We were asking the board the usual silly questions—when we'd get married and to whom. We each took turns asking the same thing, oohing and aahing over the answers. At my turn, when I asked who I would marry; the board clearly spelled out the name David. I incorrectly assumed this was a guy in my sophomore class who I thought had a slight crush on me. I was wrong about the crush, but the board was right. Both times, as it turned out.

In high school I had a reputation I was proud of, peers knew me for my sense of humor and good grades. I was popular enough—I had four really great best friends—but I preferred keeping to myself and being off somewhere with my nose in a book. So it was surprising that I was the first of us to get married. I graduated high school at seventeen and was married three days later to the only guy I'd ever really dated, a man five years my senior whom I'd met the summer before. Mom didn't approve at all. She'd offered to take out a loan to send me on a trip around the world—send me to college so I could be a journalist for the *National Geographic*—if I'd just give back the ring. It wasn't just being seventeen and the neighbors suspecting pregnancy, it was my choice in men. We'd have enough going against us with age alone without adding cultural and religious differences. David was Japanese and had been raised in a Buddhist household. Not only was he short, he wasn't even Christian. As for him marrying a *hukagene*, his parents weren't that thrilled either. We were violating both local convention and ethnic tradition.

Ah, but we were in love, and I was all of seventeen.

David had been working for the Internal Revenue Service in Memphis throughout my senior year and after the wedding we returned there. We settled in an apartment only a half mile from Graceland, right off Elvis Presley Boulevard. There were usually tourists packing the sidewalk outside the gates, snapping pictures, hoping that the King might come out and they'd get a shot. We went by there all the time to do our grocery shopping but never stopped; we didn't want to be like those silly tourists. Then one day I told David I wanted to stop.

"Are you kiddin' me? What for?"

"Just pull over. I want to get out. C'mon, just for the heck of it."

The backstory is that back on the farm, way before I got to Memphis or ever dreamed of going, I, like a lot of other teenaged girls, had a crush on pretty young Elvis. It felt much more than a crush to me, though. That was the thing. I knew in my very soul after seeing *Blue Hawaii*, that one day Elvis would look into my eyes and I'd be the one he couldn't help falling in love with. I couldn't get that "wise men say" song out of my head for about two years. I didn't know how it would happen, but Elvis and I were destined to meet. Still, despite the adolescent fantasy, I never saw myself moving practically next door to him a few years later as anything more than coincidence. I just thought it was privately amusing.

Until this particular day. I don't want to put more spine into this than it deserves because I still don't know there was really much to it, but it is noteworthy, if only in minor fashion, to this notion of a heightened awareness I seemed to have.

So David was embarrassed to be there with me and was hanging back. He was way too cool and I was embarrassing him. But I was thinking *He's coming, Elvis is en route. If we wait a few minutes we might see him.* I wanted to hang around long enough to test my hypothesis. I got up to the gates and looked through. There was nothing really impressive to see, people were pointing up at the house—just patches of white between the trees. I searched the house in my mind, rooms that I imagined, but there was no energy. It was dim in there. *He's not even there, you dummies,* I thought at the tourists.

David wanted to go, he said I'd had my fun. "Let's go get something to eat." Then two men walked down the drive and stopped at the gates. I thought they were going to shoo us away when suddenly an excitement caught the crowd as a white limo approached. It pulled aside and turned into the drive and waited for the gates to open. I was standing right there, perfectly positioned outside the back right-side door. I could have reached out and opened the door if I hadn't been afraid someone might shoot me. I put my face up to the shaded glass as close as I dared and peered like a die-hard fan. A bolt of lightning seemed to strike me; it was a shock to the system, because it was actually *him* on the other side—just like I had predicted. He was looking straight back at me through dark glasses, seeing a country girl right off the farm. He was a country boy too. Impressions passed through the window: I was young, he was tired and lonely; he had this fine car and all these fans but nothing waiting for him up at the house. I actually felt sorry for the most famous man in the world. I sensed something was wrong with him, he wasn't who I thought he was, he was sick or wasn't thinking right. It scared me a little.

Then the limo slipped through the gates, and five years later the King would be dead.

This was probably nothing more than a strange coincidence, but it is interesting that back in the spring of 1972, before Elvis's private miseries were widely broadcast, when many still had yet to come, that I'd have picked up on them. Especially since he was at the height of his game professionally; "Burnin' Love" and "Separate Ways" topped the charts that year, and he was Vegas's biggest-ever sensation.

Now that I'd had my chance with Elvis and realized I didn't want him, it was time to get real. I wanted to pursue a career in writing, and by this time had published several children's stories in magazines like *Jack and Jill* and *Ranger Rick*. The problem was the trickling income. So at David's behest, I put in my application at the IRS and was waiting to be called for a job as a tax examiner. In the meantime,

I had a lot of time on my hands; tending our tiny second-floor apartment didn't take much of the day, and I was far away from home and without friends who might have prevented me from getting bored. I waited eagerly each day for four forty-five when David returned home.

One day began as usual. I'd cleaned most of the morning, and by one o'clock I was out of things to do. I wasn't into daytime television, and I'd exhausted my stack of paperbacks. I decided to try to take a nap so the time would go by faster. I went in and lay down atop a freshly made bed. I was thinking about Utah and was thinking about calling my mother after dinner when I heard David climbing the stairs to the apartment. His footfalls were unmistakable. How could this be? I'd just lain down. Maybe he'd taken my complaints of boredom seriously, and since it was Friday he'd cut out of work early to take me to dinner. He liked doing things like that for me when he could. He enjoyed surprising me. A few weeks ago he'd surprised me by short sheeting the bed.

Now I thought to surprise him too. I would pretend to be asleep, then jump up and scare him when he walked into the bedroom and gave me a kiss.

I listened as he put the key into the lock. I heard him enter and close the door. The frosted glass in it rattled. He must have gone to the mailbox before coming in, for he stood in the kitchen looking through the bills for a minute before coming to find me. He walked into the room, and as if he hadn't seen me lying there, walked straight to the dresser that was only three feet from the bed's end. I was a bit disappointed he hadn't come over to wake me, he was messing up my plan, but I kept my eyes closed waiting for him to turn around and give me my opportunity. I was imagining how we'd laugh about it later over dinner.

I heard him empty his pockets of change and sprinkle it on the dresser. I heard him take off his tie and remove his wallet, things I'd heard him do a hundred times. I knew he was facing the mirror and could probably see me behind him, so I kept up the pretense of sleeping. I wondered if he knew what I was up to, and if he might have been planning a counteroffensive.

Then he turned, and instantly I knew this wasn't David; it was an imposter. Someone wanted me to think this was my husband by mimicking him to the smallest detail, allowing him into my bedroom, and I'd been taken completely in until our souls met face to face. It was an *astonishing* deception. This was something bad.

He moved to the side of the bed, and though my eyes were closed, I felt his gaze on me. I felt the room fill with his dangerous presence. I was immediately aware of my vulnerability, outmatched by an omniscient mind that knew I was feigning. This thing knew all about pretense. Worse, he seemed to know about *me*. I searched for his intention and found emptiness. We probed one another as warring consciousnesses.

I knew he meant to make a move, but first he had to get me to acknowledge him by succumbing to fear; this fear was his power. He was trying to find me inside where I'd frozen, trying to get me to open my eyes and come out; maybe he needed to be invited in for whatever he had in mind to work. It might sound silly, but I knew instinctively that if I opened my eyes, I'd be abandoning my only defense, that I'd cave and be "gone," because I was staring eye to eye with a consciousness whose nerve outmatched mine. I'd be the first one to look away and that would be giving up my ground. Better not to look at all if you'd already seen it in your mind's eye. There was a great benefit in willpower because at times like this it was all I had.

My body was useless with fear but my mind was alert; I knew I had to make my move before it did, and I knew it would require more than myself to meet this challenge. Something wiser and better, with more authority in the universe than I had, an energy purer. I hadn't gone to Sunday school for nothing; I started praying my socks off. If God loved me then He must help me. I begged for His awareness. Then something entered mine.

I remembered what I'd learned in Sunday school about Christ speaking to the Tempter in the desert, I remembered what he'd said. If it worked for him … Something told me to try to sit up, to assert my physical self and to say these words *out loud;* they had to make a "dent" if I was to reclaim my territory. I struggled to get up on the pillows, but I was so intimidated that halfway sitting was all I could manage and a squeak was all that came out. "Get thee hence, Satan." These words barely breathed into audibility must have made the dent they needed to, because the instant I squeaked them, the room was "free" again. Honestly, it was like a magic spell or something.

I lay there for awhile thanking God, afraid to leave Grace's embrace. I felt sure there were angels with muscle in that tiny bedroom and I thanked them too.

The first thing I did when I opened my eyes was to check out the clock; I wanted to know if I'd really been asleep. Around ten minutes had passed, long enough to have fallen asleep, I guess, but I was too shaken in my soul to buy it. Although I understood it wouldn't return, I still had all afternoon to wait. David found me at four forty-five, sitting on the cool cement steps in the sizzling summer heat of Memphis.

Most folks I've told this story to question the demon, just as I'd have done hearing such a story prior to having experienced one myself. I'd have agreed it was a nightmare and that I was the author of the distress because folks like me think we have a choice in the matter, that if we can turn the idea of incarnate evil into superstition we can refuse its existence. But as disenchanting as it was, this experience brought me to know that, while it probably wasn't a demon in the Catholic sense, sinister beings do exist. Having this thing's personal attention turned on me, *perceiving* me while it was vacant itself, was terrifying. I remember that split second where I searched it for compassion and was mocked, not by cruel cynicism but crueler indifference; it was like arguing with a black hole over sucking you in. And this was what terrified me—this intelligence couldn't be negotiated with for it'd never been human, it was alien to the human race. Compassion was an unknown sentiment.

Who wouldn't rather shrug it off as a nightmare? It wouldn't irritate my cosmology then, and it would certainly suit my view of myself better. I'm an academic and things like this are unfashionable; no one speaks seriously of the "Devil" anymore. Why'd it have to happen to me? Shake up *my* world. Maybe I'll never know why I encountered this negative being at seventeen in a tiny Memphis apartment in the middle of the afternoon, whether it was my boredom that attracted it or it was already there when we moved in. Serially occupied living spaces can collect unwanted energy over time. But I can appreciate more about it than just surviving.

I don't want to glamorize the Bogey Man, but maybe this experience I thought I could well live without was actually some sort of necessary learning curve in my search for knowledge. It certainly broadened the understanding I had of reality as a Mormon teenager. Within Mormonism there's a tendency to only think positive, the emphasis is upon hope and good things like family and eternal glory. For me, it was always a tremendously upbeat and empowering religion. But as we tended to skirt the dark or down side of things, *this thing* informing me of the stark negativity that some intelligences embody was an upsetting surprise. Probably a necessary poke in a Pollyanna-ish eye.

This momentary spectral encounter on an otherwise innocent summer day established a fact of reality that no matter how it's handled is useful to know. It's helpful to experience the stick from both ends in order to distinguish one from the other. Knowing what angelic muscle felt like provided a memorable contrast to the gold standard of negative mystical experience this thing set. I'd call learning about a greater reality *the* learning curve, and as all these advances do, it came with benefits. Having won the tug-of-war, I took away a greater confidence in supplication that enriched my skill set. I found that prayer works like magic spells.

I'd be equipped for angels next time I needed them, and I'd be quicker on the draw if I ever had the misfortune of running into something like *it* again. Indeed, the Bogey Man provided me a basis for comparison to other suspect beings that came along later, like the ghost of a bitter old French woman who was still twenty years ahead. She wasn't exactly friendly either; she nearly radiated contempt. Still, I could see her as basically harmless, an earthbound soul who was headed for church but never got there.

This was something else.

Five

Will You Be My Mother?

By the time I was twenty-one, David and I had moved from Memphis to San Francisco, where we lived for two years before transferring to St. Paul, Minnesota. There we bought our first house, a yellow bungalow on Minnehaha Avenue. We'd both been working for the IRS, I as a tax examiner, and he as a revenue agent. I hated working there; it was always his idea because it paid well, but I wanted to try something more creative. I enjoy a good paycheck like everyone else, but it sinks in importance if I'm unhappy. I got a job as a tour guide for the Minnesota State Capitol that I really liked, but what I wanted most was to have a baby.

For some reason we had trouble with that. We hadn't used birth control for years and nothing happened. We went to all the doctors but they said we were good to go, so we kept trying.

One morning I woke up nauseated; I just knew it was morning sickness. David said not to jump to conclusions, we'd been fooled before. But I knew. Next morning was the same, and the next morning after that. It was god-awful. A week later I was at the doctor's office and it was verified. *Finally.* I resisted calling David so that I could surprise him when he walked through the door; tell him we'd done it, we were going to have a baby. I could hardly contain myself for another hour.

It was late November in Minnesota, four-thirty in the afternoon. I was sitting in a rocking chair in our living room where the sun had just gone down, slowly taking a cold pink sunset with it. I was thanking God for this child inside me when I had the impression the sun was coming back up. I saw light through my closed eyelids, and when I opened them, the sun I'd just watched set *was* coming back up over the horizon and *into the room.* I wondered if there'd been an explosion or something. I wondered if I should take cover.

I didn't have time to appreciate how truly odd it was before I saw in this column of light two women—they were surrounded by whiteness as if carried by it. I remember that their feet drifted about two or three feet above the floor so they stood just slightly higher than myself. Both were dressed in simple white gowns, but not identical. I thought it reflected taste. One was tall and slender—I recognized her immediately—the other was shorter. Petite. She was an attractive woman with straight dark hair down to her waist.

"Don't be afraid," the tall woman said. "I'm your grandmother."

"I know," I told her. Again this was all telepathic, and again I thought it silly that she should bother to introduce herself. But I didn't know this other woman who stood beside her.

"This woman wants you to be her mother," Grandma explained. "Will you be?"

I remember thinking it a dumb question. "Yes, oh yes!" I answered with my heart, and with it they were gone; wonderful, yet disappointing. It'd seemed rather practical, like they'd come to make an agreement official and that was it. The place was dark now, night had come on. I got up and switched on some lights, and when David came through the door I was jumping up and down with our news. We were having a baby, a baby *girl*.

And we did. On July 22, Jill Sumiko came into this world.

Now the thing I found most intriguing about Grandma's second visit wasn't the appearance of two ghosts in my living room but their business. It surprised me that my baby would have to ask me to be its mother, it made me wonder if I'd asked my own mother, but this agreement was certainly meant to show me that we do have choices in our relationships and one must acknowledge that being choices, they have design. One might call what Jill and I agreed to as part of a designer soul plan. This involves the concept of each of us setting our own terms for incarnation by providing ourselves the right physical stage with the relevant growth circumstances, and the right characters that will help us choose the best possibility out of all those given us in the flesh, if we remain loyal to the plan. These designs-for-growth experiences take shape in the form of man and aren't slated but blueprinted in a preexistent state before each lifetime.

This was Grandma Fluhman's second and last visual appearance. For some reason our relationship didn't depend on being alive at the same time and it involved only two visits that I'm sure of. I'd had as hard a time trying to figure out why she stopped appearing as Mom did explaining why she had appeared to me in the first place. I was curious to know myself. What did we mean to each other? As she was a connection between Jill and me, she must be part of the plan too; it would explain why I'd felt I'd known her forever and why introductions seemed superfluous.

Though I recognized her on both occasions I knew nothing about her, and in my investigation I found that few did either, even Mother. Grandma was a little bit of a mystery woman. Grandma was born Harriet Ann Richards and was described by those who knew her as a tall, slender, dark-haired woman who loved to travel and experience the world but kept to herself. She was born in Indiana, worked a while in Michigan, and in her thirties ended up as a writer for a Colorado newspaper. It was there she answered Grandpa's classified ad for a mail-order bride; that's how she ultimately wound up on a Utah apple farm. Her being a mail-order bride always intrigued me, she'd either been desperate or she'd been gutsy. Mom often told me I reminded her of her mother by the things I'd say. She said our minds worked in similar ways.

But for me that wasn't good enough to explain our connection, because Grandma hadn't come to casually hang out or check in with a granddaughter, she'd been the bearer of big news on a hot topic. Her two jars established existence like bookends. She'd been there to comfort a child's first conceptualization of death and inform it, assuring me at an age when death was hardly an interest that there was nothing *to get* worried about. Whatever there ever was of a person was still there after death. This was privileged information about man's biggest question and she brought it specifically to me. Why had she wanted me to know these things? Why didn't my friends' grandmothers tell *them*?

Before this I was innocently oblivious to problematic things, as children raised in loving circumstance are. I knew all about the resurrection and spiritual beings like angels in the Bible stories, but I'd not seen such glorious beings myself; just Grandma, my very own relative. It made heaven personal. I owed it to myself to learn just what was really going on; experience hits home much better than anecdote. How was this actually happening? Why me?

Later on, I learned by looking into her genealogy that Grandma was Welsh. The finding doubled my Celtic blood and pointed to a possible affinity; maybe I'd inherited my spiritual abilities from her and she wanted me aware of them. Our minds worked the same way, maybe that's why she chose me. Rather than the boisterous Irish of my father's line to whom I'd always granted ancestral honors for my sensitivity, it was possible, and even seemed more likely to me, that if my ability was a spiritual inheritance it would come from this quiet, intensely private, mystery woman. Mother said we were so alike that, although it had hurt her feelings a bit when I'd first reported Grandma's visit, the more she thought about it, it sort of made sense.

The why of Grandma may not be important. But what she left me with is. Both the truth she bore of wider reality and the value of a personal testimony of it in my life, have been boons to my existence.

Her message was not to worry, that as I grew up I'd be exposed to all sorts of confusing attitudes about the afterlife—philosophies that denied an afterlife by reducing it to superstition or wishful thinking, but I wouldn't get caught in that trap now that I *knew* better. I'd seen the proof with my own eyes. It was comforting and saved me a lot of time.

Grandma squashed a fear of death even before one could seed, and she replaced it with a head start. Then she gave it some direction. Not only did her appearance at the bedside right after viewing her body in the ground shatter the myth of death but, at that instant, presented a whole new frontier to explore. At eight you don't expect for one-time things like this to have an impact. But it was around this time that I began fancying the mysterious and experimenting with the unseen, amusing myself with activities like locating light bulb strings immersed in darkness and receiving messages in closets and shoe boxes.

These tests of intuition were fueled by experiences that later on begged to be looked at. No doubt they had a part in my decision to study anthropology, where I could find many different lenses. The choices I've made in life have been my own, but Grandma was the different drummer I've always had to reckon with. Persuading a life's course is a profound responsibility, so if, as this second visit implied, we chose significant relationships as part of a prearranged plan to some good end, then Grandma's two appearances were somewhere in a contract.

I can't say we all have the chance to pick our parents, friends, lovers, adversaries, and kids, but I know that Jill chose to go through life with me. Today, in her thirties, she's a petite woman with straight dark hair halfway to her waist, the very image of Grandma's companion. Amber has sometimes considered it a slight that she had no prenatal introduction like her sister, but I tell her she didn't need one. I'm not convinced that Grandma brought Jill to seal some deal; I have a feeling we'd already agreed because neither of us are the kind to wait until the last minute. I think it was just the perfect time for Grandma to make a point about reality.

I used to think a lot about these chosen spiritual arrangements when the girls were going through the *Sturm und Drang* of their teenage years, only reminding them of it when I was down to the last straw. But neither of them could buy it. They weren't stupid. If they could have picked their parents they'd have picked rich ones.

Six

The Ceiling Ghosts

In the next few years a lot happened. We moved from Minnesota to Jackson Hole, Wyoming where David quit the IRS to start his own accounting business, then back to Utah, where Amber was born and David and I divorced a year later. Afterward, I sent myself to college. A month before graduation, Mom died. Several weeks later, the girls and I were on our way to Massachusetts where I planned to enter graduate school in anthropology that fall. Having grown up with my head in a *National Geographic,* I imagined the rest of me in one someday, and of course, by now I'd developed a personal interest in the variety of human experience that anthropologists studied. UMass had a good reputation for the social sciences, and I chose the Amherst campus because it was rural; nestled in the Berkshires, it seemed the best place for kids.

We'd been there about two and a half years when one morning I awoke out of the fog of a dream and sensed Mother. I lay there trying to retrieve the details, thinking it *must* have been about her, but the day had already seeped into consciousness and recapture was hopeless. I remember that it was June, the girls were in Utah visiting their father and I'd been missing them. I suppose that's why I was thinking the big house we rented was far too quiet to feel comfortable.

I got up and immediately went to the room's second-floor window. It overlooked Massasoit Street in Northampton, an upscale residential neighborhood of Victorian houses across the mansion-lined road from Smith. How the girls and I came to live in Calvin Coolidge's summer home is not important here, but the setting is significant because I appreciated how somewhere in the thirties Coolidge himself had probably stood in that very spot. I was sort of standing in his shoes, and I got to smiling about why they called him Silent Cal. I wondered if Calvin felt out of place, if he was as uncomfortable in the White House as I had become in his house. I wondered if he was the presence I sometimes felt when I took the back staircase to the third floor; it was isolated up there and I wondered if he used to go there to think.

I tried again to recall the conversation I'd had with Mom before waking up, somehow my thoughts about the reticent president had redirected me to her. I felt nagged by the idea that I was supposed to remember some important advice I'd been given just before I woke up. No dice. I then began to wonder what I was going to do with my day, another day without my young companions. If Jill and Amber had been there it would have been a good day for flying kites in Child's Park, or maybe take a drive and explore the area. I suddenly had the idea to take a drive myself. Maybe just out to Quabbin Reservoir, or up north into southern Vermont, somewhere away from Calvin's big old empty house.

A couple of hours later I was far from Quabbin and headed the other direction; I was touring the Massachusetts coast. I drove to Maine and then up its coast. Something told me I'd like to live there. I started to think about it. I was as far as Kennebunk when I *first* told myself it was time to double back, but I kept following the dotted white line north. I'd go as far as Bath, then turn around. After Bath I decided to go to Portland, then, the next town. After that one I thought, *Just let go, you'll know when it's time. You don't even know what you're looking for.*

I arrived in the midcoast village of Searsport around a quarter to five and parked in a local realtor's lot. Under ordinary circumstances I'd never approach anyone so late in the day when they're anxious to get home to dinner, but these didn't seem like ordinary circumstances. I was uncharacteristically emboldened, entering the door as the small blond realtor was turning off the light.

I made a sincere apology then got straight to the point. What did they have around there that I could afford? I only needed two things: to be close to the water and to have a fireplace. Surely there was something. I had a down payment.

There was something. She turned the light back on and told me about a place put on the market only yesterday; she hadn't even written it up yet. She handed me a picture of a sorry-looking farmhouse. She called it a "great old Victorian fixer-upper with a barn and two acres, a fireplace, *and* water views!" How lucky; it seemed just the ticket.

"How old?" I asked.

"Really old"—but that just meant charming in realtor talk—"1860 actually, the year the Civil War began." In fact, the house was just up from the harbor where the old nineteenth-century shipbuilding pier had supplied half the North's navy. Stockton Harbor had once been a hub of activity; nothing but pilings left now. The house had been built by a shipbuilder's apprentice and part-time farmer. "It comes with history."

I asked if I could go out and have a quick look, truly ashamed of myself for asking, but she'd been feeding my interest. She knew I had money, so she had no problem with it.

We drove north to Stockton Springs, a village on Penobscot Bay. Halfway down to the shore off Pogey Point we arrived at a white clapboard "ghost." There was a barn and tack shed ghost too. A cedar-shaked potting shed was more a skeleton. She was right, the place had "fixer upper" scribbled all over it, but she pointed out its bones—its three sturdy chimneys, and how firm the granite foundation still was. And wood gutters! "Oh my, no one has those these days, you can't buy that kind of charm and there's not a whisker of rot!" The place was Currier & Ives. The oaks and maples were impressively mature. Nice neighborhood. Good people. *C'mon, it's almost six o'clock.*

I hadn't planned on buying a house before sunset, but there you have it. That's how I spent my inheritance without thinking twice about it.

I awoke the next day surprised at myself. I'm not typically an impulse shopper, especially when it requires fifteen grand down, and I didn't even know the place I was moving my family to. What had come over me yesterday? What if it didn't turn out? I'd felt sure it had been the right thing to do on my drive back, but now I was sobered by the commitment and the thought of another big transition. Removing the kids from school, uprooting them from their friends and my career connections, made this sudden switch of track seem like a terrible derailment. I hadn't planned to live in Massachusetts forever, but I hadn't planned on leaving it this early.

And I'd made a promise. The promise not to touch the money unless it was for something Mom would approve of. It was a small amount as inheritances go—nothing extravagant—but it was dear, dear to her because it came from the sale of her parents' home and twenty-four acres; dear to me because they were my stomping grounds too. It was like selling one's roots. If I was going to trade a memento like that it would have to be for something of equal value, and there I was, barely able to recall the place except that it needed work. It was as if I'd sleepwalked into the purchase.

The idea to leave when I was just beginning work on my doctorate seemed pure folly up until that day, and a wondering mind had to ask if its changing into necessity had anything to do with the farmhouse in Maine going up for sale less than twenty-four hours earlier. The money sat quietly accruing interest for three years until that morning; not until Ed Larabee's widow signed with a realtor did it start burning a hole in my pocket. If it was just coincidence, it was a dramatic one, starting with that compulsion to take a drive. Who gets in a car and wanders aimlessly into the next chapter of their life, in one day and without an ounce of forethought? If not dramatic, it was uncharacteristically reckless of me.

I don't feel I need to exonerate my risk-taking by suggesting Mother made me do it. I'm a big girl and can take responsibility for my decisions, but I honestly think she had a hand in it somewhere. Maybe having second thoughts at the time about this major life change was the reason I felt she was a co-conspirator from the start, maybe she was a convenient way to justify my impulsiveness and make me feel better about the little fixer-upper in the boondocks. But I somehow *knew* better; Mother's involvement seemed real and the reason for it obvious. We'd had a silent understanding about the money; it was to be earmarked for a home-court advantage in the world: roots. For Mom a strong sense of place was important, so it didn't seem so unlikely that the sense of sleepwalking came from following some otherworldly GPS across two states and straight to the door of a sorry-looking little farmhouse that was waiting for me, and has given me twenty-five years of roots since.

It seems a bit fantastic to think Mom picked out the house that Hyrum Crooker built in 1860 on Pogey Point, but I immediately synched with the sorry-looking farmhouse in an obscure little town on a spicket of land named after fish bait. Somehow this spot was, and still is, right on the money, and the odds of me just up and finding the perfect fit in one day, the first and only prospect considered, seems as remote as finding a soul mate before sunset. I was either exceptionally lucky or I was inspired to find the two acres with its house, barn, tack and potting shed, completed somehow with an apple orchard. I was either lucky to have found a place that lived up to my memento in one shot, or I was guided. The mountains were exchanged for the sea and the brick for clapboard, but it was the right spot to re-root and perpetuate home.

Even if it was haunted, people need a sense of place.

Now I don't know if Crooker's was haunted before we got there, but it certainly possessed a feature that may lend itself to activity—an earthen cellar, which has water running through it as part of the watershed design. Whether this was planned or just the way the water wanted to go, the eight-inch-deep riverlet marks an east-to-west course. Moving water generates an electromagnetic field and a charged environment is thought to be more conducive to paranormal activity. Since water had been trickling beneath the house since Crooker's day, the place might have held the potential for paranormal activity, though Ed and Annie Larrabee had lived in it for the prior forty, as far as I knew, uneventful years.

While the yard and fruit trees were untended and the house needed paint and the barn leaned, it didn't necessarily look or feel like a haunted place. It just looked to me like it *could* one day be a bright and beautiful place. I wasn't afraid of putting the work into it; whatever a man could do I could probably learn to do with a few power tools.

I didn't get the vibe it was haunted until the hauntings actually began, so maybe the activity all started with us. Maybe all that potential energy generated by the watershed went untapped until I moved in with my sensitivity and the energy of two healthy kids. Maybe we put a spark into the bones of the house, brought it back to life after years of not knowing youth. Considering its past ownership, it might have been as far back as Old Hyrum's day since there were kids in the house.

The first haunting actually began in the old Victorian nursery. It was off the master bedroom that I'd made into my study, and when I began writing my dissertation I spent a lot of time there; Jill and Amber were constantly complaining about it. Long into the evening, sometimes through the night, I carved away at a social deconstruction of Gypsy taboo based on the fieldwork I'd been doing with a family in Boston. Then, too tired to go downstairs to the bathroom to pee or brush my teeth, I'd simply make it around the corner and fall into bed.

I had done this very thing one night when something woke me. I had the sense that something was going on in my study. I heard movement, like a swish of papers or the sweep of pages in a book left open. I thought one of the girls might have gotten up and gone to find me, but the light wasn't on, and they'd certainly not be rummaging through my papers. Then I heard the unmistakable creaking of my writing chair, an old Windsor, and I had the impression that someone was sitting there reading what I'd written from the dark computer screen. *Someone's sitting in my chair*, I thought, *like Papa Bear. Somebody's interested in what I'm doing from morning to night in the former nursery.*

I ran a list of suspects through my head. Maybe Hyrum Crooker—the guy who had built the room for a child on the cusp of the Civil War—was snooping around. He might have been confused to find a computer instead of a cradle there. Maybe it was Ed who'd "rather go fishin' than paint," a complaint voiced by his widow to account for the house's condition. Ed had died in the downstairs front parlor, but I had a feeling he'd still rather go fishin' than stick around the house. Maybe Mother or Grandma were checking in.

"Hello," I called out. "Are you there?"

I really didn't want anyone to answer; I hadn't prepared for step two and I was really tired, so I was glad when no one did. I tried sleep again, hoping whoever it was was good at editing. I had a doctoral committee meeting the following week.

I heard this nosy ghost sitting in the Windsor several more times. One of those times, I snuck around the corner to see if I could catch them and felt like a dummy afterward for being scared of a dark room. After the fourth or fifth time I was questioning this trespass out loud; I wanted to know who was sitting in my chair eavesdropping on my day—whether it was a previous owner or a complete stranger. If this spirit was singular to the house then I'd probably never attach a sure identity, but if it were personal, someone I knew, then the most likely suspect would be Mother. I suspected she was familiar with the house that had a brook running through it.

Mother was my prime suspect, though the more I thought about it the less it seemed the kind of thing for her to do. She would not be the kind to sit down and read an ethnographical analysis in order to check up on me. It wouldn't be her way. This was more likely a stranger, perhaps a Gypsy who was interested in what in-house secrets I was telling; a taboo that I'd been warned could have consequences like visits from the Gypsy dead, if broken. I figured that trying to narrow it down to a particular spirit was useless; it could have been *anyone* dead.

I'd assumed it was a single individual as the sounds were always the same. This routine never changed: the paper swishing, pages turning, the creaky chair. But it got bolder. Sometimes I wasn't even asleep before I heard the rustling, sometimes it started before I'd even turned out the light, while I was still up and reading in bed. It seemed as time went on the snooper didn't care to be sneaky—I guessed there was no need to bother if I already knew. This snoopy ghost seemed harmless enough, but the next time it happened I spoke up and asked whoever was there to explain themselves. If they were alright with my knowing about them, why didn't they appear, or say something? *Only if they were decent, though!* I added as a telepathic postscript from the safety of my bed. No negative beings allowed.

The nursery went quiet after that. I didn't think it was because there was a negative entity reading through my field notes. I didn't think its nature was the issue. Getting in my face seemed to be the intent, because the bedroom assumed the problem. I'd gotten my wish for better communication, I guess, because not long after making the request I began hearing voices coming from the bedroom ceiling. I'd awake around three, the dead of night, hearing mumbled conversations. It wasn't one individual, now there was a literal party. The voices came through as cocktail party talk muffled through a wall. The source was the upper left-hand corner of my bedroom doorway that leads into the hall and down the stairs. This stairway area has been a center of mysterious activity ever since.

One night I woke up frozen to the pillow; there was whispering in the room and my body had reacted before consciousness had. The whispering was coming from above the doorway and I suddenly found myself eavesdropping on a conversation between these unknown invisible people. I scanned with my intuition to see if I could identify anyone. Nobody registered, so I tried to get the gist of what they were saying, trying to learn why they'd picked my bedroom to party in. I waited them out in cold fear, listening but understanding in vain. I wondered if they knew I could hear them. I couldn't tell what they were gabbing about, but it seemed irrelevant to me. They seemed so indifferent that I wondered if they'd overlooked the divide and had drifted beyond the pale. Maybe if I pretended the same disinterest they'd go back where they belonged and I could get some sleep.

But they didn't. They kept coming as if my denial of them was an open welcome. I felt some challenge in it as it assumed regularity; I was awakened like this every couple of months.

Then it got personal. I awoke around three to the cocktail crowd one night, and by now seeing it an affliction, I was determined to establish who these people were and what their business with me was. There was a man and a woman, but there were others in the background. "*She knows we can see her,*" one whispered. It chilled me because they had been ignoring me and there was safety in it. Now I had their full attention. I knew they were watching me and from the tenor of the moment they seemed to be amused by the situation, indifferent to my fear and lack of comprehension. They seemed to be waiting to see what I'd do now that we'd formally acknowledged each other.

The next morning I went over to the lighthouse and had coffee with my best friend Ruth at the Keeper's Cottage B&B. Ruth had familiarity with these matters. The Keeper's Cottage was haunted by unseen guests that gave the living guests bad dreams. There were complaints of distant shouting, footsteps pacing in the kitchen, and discussions overheard in empty parlors. A retired admiral who'd stayed there took a photo of the lighthouse and cottage and was puzzled by an anomaly against the white wall that connected them; a shadow roughly human size and shape that shouldn't have been there that time of day.

Bad dreams and a poor night's sleep weren't good for business, so Ruth had a cleansing ceremony. "Just tell 'em next time to go. Assert your jurisdiction," Ruth advised me. "You're in control."

Yeah, I'd forgotten that lesson. Memphis was a long time ago.

These ghosts didn't seem dangerous like that thing in Memphis had been, but I couldn't take chances—I had two daughters to protect and I couldn't gauge the mood of the situation. Though I didn't sense harm, I had some resistance to accepting their intrusion as innocent; they seemed to enjoy startling me and having the leg up. And they were repeat offenders. It might have been fun for them but it wasn't good behavior. I needed them gone for the sake of our household.

The cocktail crowd held off coming again for a while. Maybe they knew I'd evict them. It was almost six months later when they woke me again, and as I'd rehearsed in my head, I sat up in bed and firmly but reasonably sent them on their way.

The next time I was invited to a ghost party was in Canada. By this time I was in my midthirties, had received my doctorate, and was working on the Orono campus of the University of Maine where my team had a grant to design and implement a distance education program for master's level nurses. We were three anthropologists trying to squeeze cultural understanding into a biomedical model, and trying to demonstrate the effectiveness of online courses in far-flung places.

Shortly after getting to Maine I began dating Jack, a dentist with a son and daughter who were the same ages as Amber and Jill. Though we never combined households in the decade we were together, we enjoyed a strong sense of family. The six of us spent holidays together, went on skiing and sailing trips, celebrated birthdays and graduations, and supported each other at swim, soccer, gymnastics, and cheerleading meets.

Jack and I were traveling fools. If we weren't planning an overseas trip, we were planning a road trip. We shared a love for exploring New England B&Bs, out-of-the-way restaurants, and discovering new wines. It was all rather romantic and exciting. On this trip, we were touring eastern Canada on our way to Cape Breton. The first night we stayed in New Brunswick where Jack had booked us a room at the Palmer House Inn, an impressive Victorian town house built by a British doctor in the 1880s. We checked into the Lady Palmer suite, and after a lovely dinner and a stroll down to the water, we went back to our room and went to bed.

I was to play the princess and the pea all night. At first it was just a restless tumbling to get comfortable in a foreign bed, but by two o'clock it had become less a struggle with a luxury memory foam mattress than with the luxury room. Maybe it happens in all Victorian structures, but this place had ceiling ghosts too. I didn't think they were the same ones that haunted my bedroom, but they were at a similar gathering, and as before, this party was bleeding into our world through the ceiling above a doorway. This door once annexed the room on the other side of the wall and was locked. An armoire was set against it.

These Canadian ghosts were quite a bit noisier than the ones at my house. They were much more careless, if not deliberate, in being overheard; maybe they knew I'd had practice, or maybe I was just getting better at it. I got up and walked to the wall where the voices seemed to be coming from. I even knocked on the wall in case the sounds were from people in the other room who needed reminding it was time for sleep. I had the feeling the ghosts were amused by this, probably had watched lots of people come and go in the Lady Palmer suite, and watched lots of them pound on the wall.

I opened the door that led out into the hall, went and stood outside the door of the adjoining room, and put my ear to the door. I couldn't hear anything out in the hall, but when I got back into bed they were partying again. I got the impression they enjoyed annoying us, but maybe I was just projecting. I lay there wondering what would happen, if this would continue all night. I didn't feel right demanding they go because this was more their space than mine. I felt it would be human arrogance and I didn't want to piss them off. They weren't harming anyone. I just didn't know *why* I could hear them—if it was a slip on their part or if it had something to do with me. I didn't want to be crazy. Once again, I tried gathering the drift, and once again it was too mumbled to make out. I decided it was a good thing. Psychotics usually get clearer messaging.

I watched Jack's fitful struggle to sleep. At one point he got up to take a Benadryl to facilitate it and I asked him if he heard people mumbling. "Is that what it is?" he asked about what was keeping him in a half-state of sleep. He told me to call the manager or go bang on the wall again to get them to stop. It was nearly three in the morning.

The next morning he awoke in a bad mood, not particularly uncommon for him, but this he blamed on the cramped bed, the cramped room, though neither was, they just had that feeling. "Did I get any sleep?" he asked, as if my job was to watch over him.

"You slept," I told him, "just not very well. I'm the one who was awake all night." I reminded him about the disembodied voices. He said he was sure they had bodies, it was just that sound traveled better at night; they might have been coming from the pub down the street. I said it would make perfect sense if there actually *was* a pub down the street, but it seemed to him an unimportant detail.

At breakfast we were served by a handsome male waiter who invited conversation, so I asked him if he could check with the desk to see if the room next to ours had been occupied. He reported back that only Lady Palmer's suite had been, that we'd been alone on the second floor. It was April and he said that most tourists hadn't shown up yet. I recalled that when we'd checked in we'd been told as much.

"Is that room haunted?" I asked, causing Jack to flinch.

I knew it was when the kid smiled at the question instead of acting surprised. I mentioned our experience, which didn't faze him. Instead, he told me about the original owners. Although Dr. Palmer had built the fine old house, he was seldom there, often being away for long periods of time, which was hard on Lady Palmer. She became a socialite to deal with her loneliness. Our waiter, along with everybody else that worked there, had come to the conclusion that the good lady was still entertaining friends.

As far as most accounts go, spirit would rather be heard than seen, making this a somewhat typical ghostly experience. Some in the field attribute these types of sounds to residual energy, in this case a conversation that took place in the past that's stuck in the horsehair plaster and lath, the pumpkin pine floors, the 153-year-old energy field. Residual haunts are phenomena confined to the structures, allowing ghosts like Lady Palmer & Friends corroboration by modern guests.

I could put the Palmer haunt down to residual energies left on the second floor—the party scenario fit—but I couldn't so easily dismiss the Crooker farmhouse this way because it was an unlikely party scene, and the house didn't jell with these characters. Plus, residual energy can't be directed, it can't respond to the request to go away—that calls for intelligence. "*She knows we can see her*" was a direct reference to me—tantamount to throwing down the gauntlet, which meant there were "ghosts at work." Although they were similar, Crooker's and the Palmer House hauntings seemed two qualitatively different cases.

Having decided upon the nature of the Crooker farmhouse haunting, I set out to determine a point to it. Experience had suggested that if it was a real haunting—an intelligent one—there usually was a point. Grandma had confirmed the soul's continuous existence, a young mother had used a shoebox to get my assistance for her newly orphaned child, and the Bogey Man had widened my view of reality, teaching me the power of prayer and the importance of vigilance. So what was the point of the ghosts that drifted in and out like a Cheshire Cat?

I went back to the one thing I heard clearly. "*She knows we can see her*" didn't have to convey some ominous advantage the ghosts had over me—it could have meant there'd been progress. If I separated my initial fear of being intruded upon by unseen strangers in the middle of the night, I sensed they enjoyed acknowledgment. As no message was ever conveyed, I have to think they were gregarious souls who found amusement in their circumstance by seeing if they could connect with someone on this side who had the receptive ability.

Seven

Ambushed by Angels

This next jar holds bolder things, like angels. I guess it might sound offensive to jar an angel; it might sound offensive to call them mere ghosts. Anyway, this is a story about spirits that acted like angels.

I didn't see the end of Jack and me coming, so when it did I was set back a bit. It was also a rather blunt blow, which made it harder to deal with. At this time I was in my early forties. Jack was approaching fifty and wrestling with the idea that there might still be a better prospect out there for him. Ideally, she'd come equipped with a trust fund, or at least more stability than a social scientist enduring periods of unemployment. Since our grant at the university had run out I'd been scrambling to find work in Maine as an anthropologist. As there was little call for them even within academia,

I finally landed a middle management job at a local mental health center, and a few years later found a teaching position in alternative education that suited me better but paid half as much. Jack was skeptical that I'd ever get secure footing working for lowly nonprofits, though I provided well enough for my own household; however, just hearing about how I did it wore Jack out. And of course, there was that midlife itch for novelty.

Though I appreciated Jack's directness later, at the time I was wrecked, stunned that this was the depth of our relationship for him after all our time together. I'd been more or less jilted because I was too poor for Jack, who'd been born with a silver spoon that entitled him to something better. Rejection on such vulgar grounds was difficult to accept, but the loss of family made it an even bigger matter. I'd grown to love Jack Jr. and Jenny, and they had grown attached to us. For Jill and Amber, they were surrogate family. It was a big, awful adjustment for everybody.

A decade was a long time to call things to a halt, and when the depression lingered on uncomfortably I entered therapy to gain some resilience. Because I lived in a relatively small place where most local therapists were people I knew from working at the clinic, I chose a therapist an hour away in Augusta. His office was the bottom floor of an office complex that fronted a side street. It was midwinter; we'd had a lot of snow and there were six-foot-high dirty snow banks lining the capital's streets. It was dark when I arrived, just after five o'clock.

I remember crying during that session, something I'd never done before in therapy; usually I'm the self-controlled type. But this therapist was breaking me down, goading me with reasons I should move on from a place of hope—resistance, refusing to let go—that was holding me up. Thinking it different was easier than making it so. He repeated the same things Ruth at the Keeper's Cottage and my sister, Judy, told me: that Jack wasn't going to make a U-turn after saying what he had, and I shouldn't want the narcissist even if he did. Where was my self-respect? I couldn't explain why I was such a mess, I just felt *broken*. It was the way everything felt.

I'm sure when time was up the guy I was paying was relieved to be through with me. I doubted this guy was the help I needed. I put on my coat and gloves, and walked out to the curb of the street I had to cross to get to my car. I saw headlights just cresting the hill to my left, but they seemed a decent distance away and the speed limit there was only twenty-five. I told myself I had plenty of time to get across as I stepped into the street.

"No you don't," I heard someone correct me, and suddenly I was back on the curb, wondering who'd had the nerve to be so familiar with me. I'd literally been yanked by the scruff of my coat and scarf. In seconds headlights barreled past, splashing icy slush onto the sidewalk, spraying my coat and boots with road salt solution. Reassembling myself, it dawned on me that death had just come calling, that if I'd crossed the road I'd now be thirty feet down it crumpled in a snow bank. The thrill of a close call warmed me, especially when there was nobody to thank for my rescue. No one was visible, but someone *was* present. I said a sober "thank you" to the personage I felt standing to my left side a little behind my shoulder, marveling that these clichéd things actually happened.

Then things became clearer, and really confusing. I recognized Death's chariot.

Although there were plenty of brown Jeep Cherokee's on the road at the time, the one that nearly mowed me down was *Jack's*! Ginger, his Golden retriever, was licking the way-back window. I waved at her and she responded by leaping from one side to the other and barking. Jack's brake lights came on as he approached the intersection where he stopped for the light. Yeah, there was the Thule box; there weren't too many of them around at that time and Jack was the type to have the first of everything.

I was trying to make sense of all this because it seemed too much of a coincidence. My humble little brain couldn't quite process it. If it wasn't "just one of those things," *which it wasn't*, then it would have to be ... *deliberate!* That sent my mind rattling. Jack had his quirks, but he was essentially a moral man, he was a doctor, a healer, at heart still a Quaker. Jack didn't have either the character or the motive. I had to acquit him simply because he couldn't have known I was in town and that I had entered counseling with this particular clinician. He couldn't have known, or cared, about the precise spot and time to run me over. Nonetheless, it felt more than a freak coincidence, it *felt* deliberate.

I wondered if Jack was looking out his rearview mirror, if he could have possibly recognized me from my coat, or if he just saw some woman his dog was barking at standing beneath a streetlight. Then the light turned green and he continued on around a corner. Jack hadn't been looking back at all.

This was one of those experiences that was so unlikely to happen, it couldn't help but carry great personal meaning. It was such a shock that it literally fogged my mind, and because it required an extra dimension to explain it, my disbelief prevented any clear comprehension of it. I couldn't really formulate a question, much less an answer. I just felt assaulted, rescued, and numb.

I sat in the car waiting for it to warm up, trying to absorb what had happened. It was ominous and to the point. Direct, the way Jack had been, the way the therapist and my best friends were trying to be. Our stretch was over and even if it wasn't, it had to be. I hadn't wanted to believe that Jack was as shallow as my pockets, that he didn't value me much more than what was in them, but whether or not I believed it, Jack's chapter was over because I couldn't argue with this message, I didn't have the energy. The reason I'd cried earlier was because I was tired. I thanked whoever it was that saved my life from the literal, if not spiritual death, of an inappropriate lover, and then asked them to help me come to terms with it. Help me heal my sorry self so I could move on and turn a corner too.

I was heading back home when I remembered a request for orange juice Amber had made before I left home. Damn. I just wanted to get back to my nest and out of the cold. I'd been doing a lot of processing; I just wanted to go light the fire, pat the dogs, and have a glass of wine. But I'd feel bad about myself if I got there empty-handed. I'd been trying harder to keep the smaller promises.

I went to Hannaford's against my will. I'd been crying, hadn't washed my hair in three days, and hadn't dressed for shopping in the "big city." In other words, I looked a mess and, always having been self-conscious, didn't want to risk running into somebody I knew. But it *was* nearly six-thirty on a cold winter's weeknight in Augusta—the parking lot was virtually empty with these temps. I glanced into the rearview mirror and saw what a horror I was, but guessed I could sacrifice my pride so Amber could have orange juice in the morning.

The store wasn't doing much business that night. The teenaged cashiers, who had nothing to do, turned to greet me. I lowered my swollen eyes and headed down some aisle just to find cover. I was a tangle of emotions and a knot in my head was forming into a headache. I had to sort myself out so I parked in the empty baking aisle and tried reckoning this peculiar brush with death. I happened to be facing the Pillsbury Doughboy on a muffin box, so I asked him if I'd just imagined it. I *had* just walked out the door of a therapist who'd brought me to tears, stepping out of his usual disaffected role to practically screech what an emotional hazard to me this man of fickle heart was—then old Fickle Heart comes along and nearly irons me flat. How could I explain that?

Now I'm talking to the Sunkist Raisin girl, a short stroll down from the muffin mix. I thought it better to keep moving to prevent calling attention to myself. I ask Raisin girl if such things really happen by chance. What were the odds that Jack and I would be out on a winter's night that most had abandoned, and with the streets virtually empty of humanity, collide in one spot for one dreadfully clarifying instant? Raisin Girl didn't know the odds, but I knew they had to be slim.

I moved on to the cornstarch, there was a cute little Indian girl on the bright yellow box. I switched gears and asked her if I was really the fool that Ruth and Judy said I was. Somehow I felt I'd been shocked into asking whether I was a modern Pollyanna when it came to my expectations about love, if old-fashioned values of respect, appreciation, and loyalty between a man and a woman were old hat; if wanting to be loved for yourself was a fool's aspiration. I felt a cold sensation spread over me for the second time that night. The first was that blink of recognition I'd had in the street about the finality of things; this flash struck as I appreciated the futility of the ideal in a modern world. Cornstarch girl had answered my question. A fool needed to learn to live with disappointment or shed the ideal.

I became suddenly aware of a man about my age at the end of the aisle wheeling his cart my way. *Oh God, why this aisle?* It happened to be cooking items, food coloring, baking soda, unmanly things like that. I asked myself if this guy was real. Did he look like the kind of guy that really baked? There was something fishy about it. Anyway, there was no reason for him to crowd me, there were twenty other aisles in this place and he was interrupting my wound licking. Making me even more self-conscious. I saw that he was good-looking and looking right at me. Our eyes met briefly. It was all I could stand, but he was smiling and inviting my attention, maybe flirting a little. I had the feeling he was trying to cheer me up but I resisted, thinking he must have been blind or had low standards. At the very least, he had very poor timing. We passed. I looked away. I was feeling anything but sociable.

I saw the meat case straight ahead and thought I'd treat the girls and myself to something special tonight. I needed something special and no price tag was fit to deter me. I was pondering the choices, picking through the steak and roasts, when this guy was suddenly there at the meat case too. Come on, there was hardly anyone else in the 60,000-square-foot store! And here he was; we were standing side by side, his cart nosing friendly with mine. I noticed there was nothing in it. What did he have—a thing for picking up sorry-looking women in empty stores on stormy nights? I was not up to this.

I was only pretending to consider the meat now, and I got the feeling he was pretending, too, that this wasn't so casual, that it was just not that *normal.* There was something unworldly about it. *He's not here alone* slipped through my mind. I had a sense that *there were others like him,* but it made no sense why I would care. Everything had taken on this surreal feel since I had walked out the therapist's door. I had to know if my intuitions were right so I dispensed with my vanity and looked at him squarely. *What is it you want?* I thought. And I thought he could hear me ask this rather direct question, but he showed no offense. He just smiled—not any smile—a delicious empathetic smile that conveyed shelter, the sort that usually came from moms, grandmothers, and true friends. I was thinking there was no reason for a smile like that, it was too familiar, but since I'd never been moved this way by a smile before I was halfway thinking of asking him if he was the angel that had just saved me. I had a feeling he hung with them. But I knew he'd heard me already and I knew he wouldn't answer even if I asked it out loud. It wasn't talk he was offering, it was approval. For some reason this complete stranger wanted me to know he cared, wanted me to lighten up, and thought that might do it.

I was unsure of this situation so I headed in the other direction. *What did I come here for anyway? Oh, the juice.*

I was at the freezer case now. I had the door open and was letting the cold air out when I became vaguely aware of two women nearby discussing something. They were about ten feet away. The place was empty when I came in—where were all these people coming from and why did they seem to be drawn to me? More than ever I needed my space. Couldn't they feel my vibe? I get grouchy when I'm uncomfortable and I was suddenly feeling vulnerable—the most uncomfortable one can get. The reality of having just dodged a bullet was finally hitting me.

I ignored the women but couldn't help overhearing some of the content as they drew closer. One owned her own hair salon and she was telling the other woman about the day she'd had, so I assumed they were friends. Then I heard one of them say, "Is it natural?" There was a pause that made me think they were referring to the orange juice and speaking to me. I was reluctant to get pulled into their conversation, but I looked up from my study of the can.

"Your hair color," the one said to me. Her cart was now right next to mine and I noticed how it was blocking me against the refrigerator case. "Is it your natural shade?"

I was thrown by this; first that anybody would be cheeky enough to ask, and second, my hair was three days dirty and flattened down from my snow cap. I told her it was; I hadn't resorted to dying yet. She laughed, too much, I think, then the other woman came closer for an inspection. "Beautiful," the salon owner said, taking the liberty to stroke a strand of my hair. It was disconcertingly *familiar.* Why were they doing this to me? I was thinking all this space and we were all bunched up in just one square of it, plus, I've got a perfect stranger pawing my dirty hair—a professional that could clearly see it was ratty. I sensed it was more than my hair they were talking about, there was another message for me behind their interest.

The salon owner released my hair. "Wish I'd been a brunette."

This was just way too weird and claustrophobic for me. I saw no reason for it. I smiled and shoved off with two cans of frozen concentrate in my gigantic shopping cart. I took the express lane even though all five cashiers were free. I was looking around. I wanted to see these people, make sure they were really here, but I didn't because the store was big and the shelving was high. I tossed around the idea of asking the clerks about these particular shoppers, but decided it would involve way too much explaining.

I sat in my car in the parking lot waiting for them. I had to know if these folks were angels, because I thought one rescued me a half hour ago, and as crazy as it sounded, I just had the feeling they weren't coming out the door, that the guy with the generous smile and the admiring ladies had left another way. Hadn't I just prayed for help in healing my sorry self? Something like that just happened in there. I felt like I'd been ambushed by angels.

After twenty-two minutes I was satisfied that I was waiting on nothing, the miracle had already happened. I felt an overwhelming need to get home to my kids and the dogs.

This was an angels-to-the-rescue story, the sort of story that was easy to slough off as wishful thinking because it invoked the idea of divine assistance, which assumed a great deal. First, that there were benevolent beings that gave a darn, second, that they gave a darn about piddly little me. For the cynic who sees piddly people everywhere, this assumes too much self-importance—the idea that the universe is sentient to man gives us humans more self-regard than we've a right to. But that seems like the same mindset that could not conceive of electricity before it was discovered, and my marketing experience would contradict that type of thinking. It seems to tell us that there's nothing piddly about a soul, particularly one that's hitting a rough patch.

Divine beings aren't required to play supporting roles at crucial points of one's life, our fellow men can and usually do suffice. But in this case I'm judging in favor of angels because it seems I needed more than ordinary human help to accept the situation and move on in a wholesome way after suffering a blow that had overwhelmed my reason. I'd misjudged what Jack and I were doing and was handling the disappointment badly, processing it too slowly for my own good. This physical demonstration helped speed that up.

Folks were right about my resistance to moving on, but talk of good reason wasn't going to cut it because that was a matter of the head; I had to *feel* the end of hope. Empathetic folks are either made this way or have this need to experience suffering to completion. Whoever orchestrated events, and I have to think it was a benevolent someone who did so simply because of the synchronicity involved—the relevance, and message, not to mention that miraculous curbside save—whoever it was, I think they had it in mind to improve on the therapeutic encounter.

Jack and I managed to preserve our friendship. Once when he was visiting I asked him about that night; I asked if he remembered nearly hitting me and then driving on. He claimed he had no memory of it; he honestly hadn't been aware he'd given me such a close call.

The personal importance of this experience can't be appreciated enough, nor can the relevance of what followed after—just asking for help to rebound.

I have good reasons for thinking the folks I ran into later weren't the usual customers. The timing and the poignancy of their kindness were suspicious after what had just happened, and I had a sense of it at the time, though not any full realization. Back when I was talking to Cornstarch girl about throwing the baby out with the bathwater and the guy turned the aisle to pick me up with that deliberate smile, it was perfect timing. I was just then making a decision, rounding a corner in attitude that I'd be left with when things straightened out again. For me it was a moment of consequence.

Besides that, and even more convincing to me, was how genuinely extraordinary these beings were. I'm not normally overwhelmed by folks at the market going out of their way to make comforting gestures. Few take the time to smile my way unless I initiate it, fewer stop to stroke my pride and lend a healing touch, and never do I invite it. It's not that we aren't good folks, we're just less mindful of one another than we probably ought to be. If this sort of magical pick-me-up was part of a typical grocery-shopping experience, then I say stick with that store.

These strangers felt suspiciously familiar enough that I sensed fiction almost at once. They weren't the ordinary shoppers, they seemed like posers. I had a feeling they were acting within normal contexts but this was temporary. The guy in the baking aisle, for example, there was subtext with him—something more was going on.

I also had the impression that the three of them were together, at least they knew one another, because I'd been aware that they'd been consulting at the meat case after I'd left, and when they disbanded the women had come my way. I realized when reliving it, that I'd been conscious of these women as presences before I actually heard or saw them, the notion that *there were others like the man with the shopping cart* registered enough so that the women's materialization strengthened my intuition that something was afoot with them and their empty carts.

Maybe it was too corny to think these peddlers of kindness were answers to prayer, placed to soften a tough corner. Maybe they weren't heavenly beings, just extra-good folks who relished bumping into pathetic strangers on cold winter nights so they could fulfill their quota of random acts of kindness for the week. Maybe it was just the ameliorating effect that talking to ingredients had on me; deciding that ideals could be negotiated with a modern world and the drive for a connection deeper than pockets was a good one to keep. Still, something more than a cute little girl on a yellow cornstarch box pulled me from the Jeep's path.

Back when I confronted the fellow at the meat case, I'd known instinctively who, or rather, *what* he was, and he knew I understood. Soul to soul, eye to eye, we were on the same page for that moment, but being a human at a personal low I asked him to confirm this. I remember feeling uneasy about it. Why would an angel bother with *me*? It was an odd thing to wonder if angels really did come around again after I had been miraculously rescued no more than twenty minutes earlier, but still, twice in one night? Twice within an hour! *What's up with these angels?*

That's what got him to smiling.

Eight

The Christmas Room Ghost

I began this memoir with my father, the Irishman whose prayers raised the dead. The one who found driving a truck suited his melancholic soul better than did farming and general contracting, or being tied to a big family. He and I had an intermittent relationship. He'd disappeared when I was three, quite literally, I'm told—his whereabouts were a mystery until he just as spontaneously reappeared when I was six, by that time needing an introduction.

One day when I was out in the front yard on a blanket with my dolls, an eighteen-wheeler pulled off the highway and parked in front of our yellow brick house. I knew the truck wasn't supposed to be parking there, it made Mom mad when people did because it disturbed her picture-window views. I thought the man in the truck was going to go across the road to Christensen's fruit stand because that's what lots of folks did. Mr. Christiansen bought up Uncle Curley's orchards when he moved to Idaho and became a millionaire growing grain, and from then on, on weekends during the peach and apple harvest, we practically had traffic jams in our front yard.

I watched to see who would climb out of the red Mack truck. I knew it was a Mack because of the silver bulldog on the engine's flattened front nose; my brothers were always talking trucks so I knew something about them. Kenworths were supposed to be the "cat's ass." I heard a big sound of air, the brakes releasing, and the driver's door finally opened and a cowboy stepped out. He was the tallest cowboy I'd ever seen, gigantic. He wore a cowboy shirt with mother-of-pearl buttons, a bolo tie with a tarantula laminated in it, big cowboy boots and a big cowboy hat, and on his big belt buckle was a scorpion. Everything about him was *big*—which made him a little scary because he came down the driveway straight at me.

I was running for cover, yelling for Mother, when he scooped me up in his big arms and lifted me into the air, then brought me down and squeezed the air out of me. His last brutal act before Mother got there was to kiss me with his big mustache that partly tickled and partly sanded off my cheek skin. I wanted to know who this guy was. He belonged to the truck, I told Mother, who laughed and introduced me to my father. "His name's Gerald," she said, "but everyone calls him Jerry." Now I could call him Dad. I remember taking a long look at him because I didn't know I had one of those. I wanted to know who he *really* was. So far I liked everything about him but that mustache.

After that, he wandered back into my life from time to time, usually whenever Oregon lumber needed hauling to Salt Lake. He'd stop by the house for dinner. On occasion I would ask if he ever thought of coming back home. Mother still loved him and he professed love for her, so what was stopping him? It was a question that always made Mom squirm, she usually ended up in the other room. "Oh, Jinnit Girl," Dad would smile, "there's things you don't understand." I guessed it was a secret, probably had something to do with "the redhead" I'd heard Judy, Dale, and Kay talking about, which later proved to be true.

I loved my dad. Mother made sure of it. Even though she vacillated between anger and forgiveness, she insisted that we not hold his leaving against him. The four older kids did and she didn't want Rod and me following suit; she said it would poison our lives. As far as I knew I didn't have anything to hold against him, there was no before and after by which to judge him. I was too young to bear a grudge and after meeting "the redhead," I really liked her.

After I married and moved East, I tried staying in touch, but Dad seemed to have no interest. He was busy with another family and was a terrible correspondent. By the time he died in the mid-nineties, we hadn't seen or spoken to one another for many years. By then my feelings for him had grown distant, by then I'd had the time to reexamine our relationship from an educated point of view and realize it wasn't what a kid deserved. Like Jack, bonding with me was an inconvenience to him. I had to soberly accept that actions spoke louder than words and concluded that I'd really never meant that much to my father. Like Jack, he just wasn't all that into me.

While he was alive I was unaware of any poison toward Dad on a conscious level, I only allowed it to register as disappointment. But a few months after coming back from his funeral I went into toxic shock. Out of the blue one day I was suddenly angry at him and feeling surprisingly hostile.

I was in the Christmas room, the parlor where we put the tree every year. The room where paint-hatin' Ed Larrabee was supposed to have died. I was dusting and got to Dad's picture on the bookcase. He was wearing a fifties hat, a fifties striped piano-key tie, and a double-breasted suit; a dapper guy who'd trade it all in for belts with scorpions and bolo ties a few years later. He was about forty-five in this picture and looking pretty pleased with himself. I wondered who the guy really was. That was all I ever really wanted to know—how the cowboy that stepped out of the Mack that day would affect me. I wasn't aware that having been disposed of at three for a Mack and a redhead had already affected me. I felt sorry for little Janet Sue in the yellow Easter dress and white gloves in the picture next to him. Then the sadness turned to anger. This hurt had a very long shelf life that surprised me. Well? Hadn't I deserved the love of my father as much as the other kids he went on to raise? What was I, disposable? All I ever wanted was his approval, and it was so elusive that it set me up for guys like Jack who never quite would approve.

I told myself not to go there, Mother taught me to overlook the ugly, but the ugly like "the redhead" was there. As I looked at my father in his prime and wished it'd gone different I knew I was facing a demon that I needed to square. I went to the window and stood staring out into a bleak spring day—the low-riding clouds were going to spring a leak any minute but I'd beat them to it. I was grieving for the unequal distribution of affection between Dad and me. I gave him unconditional love at one time; I wanted my innocence back, to feel good about loving my father, not like the fool my older siblings used to say I was. I was grieving for a life that, if he'd stayed and made good his promises, I'd have had.

In 1954 Dad was the owner of Larkin Construction. The farm provided auxiliary household income and storage space, backhoes, dump trucks, and road graders mixed easily with tractors and plows. We were doing well enough that he built the fine new brick house. Mom and Dad had many friends and the respect of the community. We were the perfect fifties American middle-class family. He'd pretty well destroyed that with his vanishing act, leaving the debts of his company behind. We went from middle- to working-class in just a few years. It was a lot for Mother to shoulder and this hardship prematurely dismantled the family. The older four cut short their youth to marry as soon as they could just so they wouldn't be an additional burden to Mom, and Rod and I both followed suit, marrying in our teens. Worse than our sudden economic decline was the impoverishment that came from being robbed of our Mother; from the time Rod and I were school age we only had her on weekends, and then she was a changed woman.

Dad pretty much wrecked our childhoods and the stress shortened my mother's life. It was no small decision and it left no small impact. I had every right to feel angry about his frailty. The tears had quit falling because I was gearing up to something. On the many times I'd asked him to explain his decision to run off, I'd received a revisionist history and came away with the idea that a man's rights outweighed his responsibilities. There was never any apology or remorse, just his annoyance at being asked and putting to use that "*there's things you don't understand, Jinnit Girl, brush off.*"

I turned back to the Christmas room and faced him.

I didn't know when he'd arrived, and what he'd heard, but he was there somewhere in the energy field. While I had his ear, I told him that neglect was one thing but making me feel unloveable was unforgiveable. I'd wasted a lot of time finding guys to prove him right. The tears came back. Why couldn't he ever say anything nice to a kid who'd loved him so much?

He didn't understand my inner outrage, so I recalled my wedding day.

We'd rented a stone chapel up Ogden Canyon near the Weber River. Dad and I were upstairs in the dressing room before the service where I was putting the final touches to myself, seated at a movie-star-lit dressing table. The time had come when the father traditionally gave the bride his blessing, but Dad thought I needed advice. He started by telling me what a fine young man David was, how he'd be a good provider. Somehow inferring, when he said I should feel lucky to have David, how damn lucky I was that I'd *ever* found a man.

Geez, I was only seventeen.

"Now Jinnit Girl, you learn to mind," he said, catching me off guard. *He was not really going to squash this moment—was he?* I didn't want to hear about my faults on my wedding day. But squash it he did. He not only told me to do whatever my husband told me to do, but to keep my big fat mouth shut and my big fat opinions to myself; David was the boss of me now. It blew me away! I had to turn and busy myself with mascara to hide the experience of spiritual annihilation. Dad went on to make his summation: David was "the one that's running the show," and I'd make him a good wife if I could learn to stay in my place. And it suddenly registered how my father saw me. A renegade woman. He didn't approve then and he never would because he didn't value me.

Crap, all I'd wanted was to be told I looked pretty.

I was holding back tears as he walked me down the aisle, angry that I allowed him to give me away; he didn't deserve me. Arm in arm we walked, with him taking credit, like he'd been there signing report cards, warding off the neighborhood boys, and getting me safely to this point. Like he knew me. "It's a sham, everybody!" I wanted to scream to the nicely seated, nicely dressed people gathered under the steeple, "This guy's a poser." This moment was so stupid I bet I will remember it the rest of my life.

"I wished I was dead on my wedding day, Dad." I spoke aloud to the Christmas room.

I knew he was listening and this was my chance to cough up all the pain of his indifference. I wanted him to account for it. I wanted it on the books. I picked his picture up and yelled to High Heaven, "*I'm not Jinnit Girl, you bastard!*"

I'd never called him that before. I remember being disappointed that it hadn't made me feel better. I needed relief and if calling your old man names didn't do it, what would?

Twelve years later, on a Sunday afternoon, I decided to take a nap. It's something I rarely do. I told David the Second, who'll be discussed in more detail later, that I was headed for a lie down, and he even commented on how unusual it was.

I hadn't been on the bed longer than a minute, in fact I only vaguely remember ever lying down, when I was just matter-of-factly in a white spacious building with endless staircases, crystal chandeliers, and lots of plate glass. There were hundreds of people there dressed in formal wear, mostly black and white, which made me wonder if I was at some black-tie gala. I don't generally feel comfortable at these types of affairs, but I was glad to be there.

I was curious about things and had no one to ask. Although the great hall was filled with people, they were all engaged, so I searched the crowd for familiar faces who could fill me in on where I was and why I was there. I had the sense that people I knew were around. Then a young man was beside me, a stranger who told me he was going to be my guide on a two-part visit.

He took me to see Mother first, her portion of the visit is described later as it was brief and not the reason for my being there. The reason I was there, the guide told me, was to see Dad. He was in a different place than Mother. It was more suited to him than Mother's world would have been.

Dad was at a park on the edge of a lake and there was a happy crowd of people. Some kids were swimming, others were running back and forth along the shore. Two boys that I sensed were brothers had a large white beach ball they were tossing back and forth. The smaller one let the ball escape him and it flew toward some woods. The older boy ran after it and passed within a few yards of me. I was surprised that spirit kids swam and ran around chasing balls; it seemed too familiar to be heaven, so I tried detecting some difference in the boy, something that made being dead different. He looked alive enough to me; I would say ordinary, except for being very happy.

I was aware that I was in the spirit world and it registered as quite an exciting privilege. I was eager to learn all I could about how things went there, but again, I had no one to ask, my guide had left me on the shore amid the picnic. Before long the anthropologist in me kicked in and I went about observing and exploring on my own, comparing features of the spirit world with those of Earth as if it were the usual fieldwork.

What struck me most was how similar things were; I felt some disappointment in it. For example, they were barbecuing. To me it came across as some sort of violation of spiritual law: ghosts didn't need to eat, did they? As any nosy anthropologist would do, I wandered over to the grill area to see what they were having. I say grill area, because it was more a grill line that stretched about forty feet. I was utterly confused to see neatly laid-out pork chops on one section, chicken and beef on others, a whole grill for hamburgers, and right in front of me were shrimp and fish. It just didn't seem right. My ideas were badly shaken. Where'd all that meat come from? Did they have slaughterhouses in heaven? I wondered if it was actual food or the remembered pleasure of it; they might not need to eat but maybe they still liked to. It would be nice to consume to your heart's content without having consequences.

I slowly became aware through the buzz around me that this was a family reunion. These happy people were my Irish kin, though I recognized no one and no one seemed familiar with me. Then a woman came up to me holding a plate, and as if I were regular, invited me to dig in. I didn't think I should as I was aware that I was not dead. I wondered if she was aware of it, and I worried that this food might not sit well with me. Everyone else was filling their plates and gabbing like there was no tomorrow. It was a regular old Larkin reunion.

Then Dad materialized from all the rest and was glad to see me. He gave me a hug and introduced me to everyone; I noticed he called me *Janet*. He even bragged about how I was an anthropologist. Then everyone lost interest and went back to merrymaking, *including* Dad. I watched him, *observed* him, I was still trying to figure out who the real cowboy in the Mack truck was. He seemed in his element here, he loved chatting with people and they all liked to laugh. But I didn't know these folks; either they'd been dead a long time or they weren't all relatives. I began wondering what I was doing there—the thought crossed my mind that I might really be dead and just not know it. I knew I wasn't in my body but was planning to return to it—but what if I didn't? What if that was it; wham, bam, thank you ma'am and you're taken off to a family reunion where you're abruptly set down with a bunch of strangers only too happy to party with or without you.

But worse: *What if that was the end of Earth for me?* The idea of it caused so much misery.

Then a blond woman whom I'd seen speaking with my dad earlier came up to greet me. I thought I'd heard her call him Uncle Jerry, so I thought I must have known her. I was trying to decide. She had blue eyes and the pointy nose and smile my older cousin Sheryl used to wear. She had Sheryl's buoyant personality and cynical laugh. She was a jovial spirit. Then she began to sing and there was no doubt it was Sheryl, that voice was the only convincing I needed. I was confused then, because as far as I knew she was still alive. Last I'd heard she was living in or around Ogden, Utah with a slew of Mormon grandkids. Uncle Rulon's side of the family stuck close to the Church; our side made better Jack Mormons.

Once I recognized Sheryl she embraced me. "How's it going?" I asked her, thinking even then it was a lame question. How *did* one greet others here? I felt a little awkward because I'd not known her well, she was my sister Kay's age, and these weren't familiar circumstances. She laughed and said things were going about the way she'd expected. I asked her if she was really dead, because as far as I knew, I wasn't. She laughed and then joked lightly about "here today, gone tomorrow" just the way I'd expected lighthearted Sheryl to do. Her cavalier attitude was always part of her charm.

Then Dad invited me to join him and a bunch of people at a picnic table shaded by an awning. For the first time I wondered where they were getting sun. It was an absolutely gorgeous light-ridden day but I didn't see the sun. There was no single direction the light came from; it was like we were the source. I overheard Dad say something about me and the Gypsies. I was surprised he knew so much about my life, especially since he never really understood what an anthropologist did, and I hadn't begun fieldwork with the Romany until after Dad had passed. I wondered, if I was to understand by his knowledge of me, if he *had been* Papa Bear in the Windsor chair rifling through my fieldwork journal and checking in with me from the computer screen. My dad loved learning and had had a keen interest in the world; for a truck driver he was a well-read man. An ethnographical analysis of Gypsy taboo might have been right up his alley.

I was introduced to one of the fellows Dad had been bragging me up to and the connection dropped. The guy smiled but didn't bother feigning interest. I could tell he was unimpressed by me and the Gypsies. I got the notion he didn't think I belonged there, so why bother? I was getting uncomfortable because I didn't see any reason to be there either. I wasn't interested in these people and they were only mildly interested in me.

That was when I noticed I was carrying a shopping bag. It had a leather coat in it that I'd gotten at some otherworldly secondhand store before getting there. It was very precious so I wanted to keep it near me, but it was a chore having to keep an eye on it with all these people. I didn't know if they had thieves in heaven, but then I didn't know they had hamburgers either. Dad warned me himself not to set the bag down or I'd lose it. He didn't want that to happen. I was surprised at his interest in my coat.

Now this next part of the experience is sketchy and relies heavily upon emotion to recall. Dad and at least two other men from the table spoke with me for a while apart from the others. The shore and picnic were gone, and we stood in a terraced place on a hill that overlooked a sprawling city; dwellings filled a valley and ascended the side of a high but gentle mountain. The city lights that designated its parameters continued beyond my view, making me wonder if this city took up a whole continent.

I couldn't fully recall the reason for this meeting, only that we discussed something important because I wouldn't have been there otherwise. The meat of the conversation has been stricken from memory—"stricken" because that's how it feels when I try to remember it, as if this memory has been denied conscious access. When I try to remember, my emotions speak of responsibility. I was either let in on some secret or I'd been given something to do, or maybe I'd made a promise. I know I'd had to agree to forget our discussion, at least for the time being, and I think I must have understood the reason for it at the time because

I was quite okay with it. I just couldn't comprehend how forgetting something important was of benefit.

I do remember our private meeting breaking up. The reason I thought something had been agreed to was because one of the men smiled at me and said, "Now don't forget." I smiled back, understanding that he was teasing me, and said I wouldn't.

It was then time to meet up with my guide. Dad reminded me to get my bag and come with him. We walked through some woods in dappled light. I was thinking they could have been the woods right across the street. There were groves of white paper-bark birches among the mixed forest, ferns and a cushion of oak and maple leaves at our feet. This unearthly sameness continued to bother me. I wasn't exactly expecting golden harps but—well, where were they?

I knew I wouldn't have the chance to speak to Dad again anytime soon, and this made me more blunt than usual. I asked him if things were different now between us. I didn't want an apology. I wanted my innocence back, my love for him justified, so I asked him the million-dollar question, which I figure he had to answer truthfully because he was in heaven. "Dad? Did you ever really love me or was I just a bother to you? You and Mom had the other four kids, it was a nice number. Was I an oops that came along nine years later, and when followed a year and a half on by another one, did you just throw your hands up in the air? Say enough is enough? *If I hadn't come along would you have stayed?*"

I remember bracing myself.

I know the question angered him, I'd hit a nerve and could hear him thinking, "Women! Why if you tell them once isn't it enough?" We'd straightened out the "oops" business before, he'd told me he and "momma" had planned on six kids from the start—she'd just needed that nine-year breather after Kent. He knew I needed to hear him give me assurance that he loved me, that he still did, but I knew he was no closer than before to feeling comfortable saying it to me and I was disappointed that things were still so awkward and difficult for him. All I wanted was one "I love you" I could trust and all I got was dead air. For once Dad didn't have anything to say and I wanted to die all over again, somehow it was worse than my wedding day.

Then I was surprised. Dad took my hand, but his comfort still came out like a scold. "Now you know I do, Janet," he said. "I can't blame you for having doubts the way things went, but don't you know in your heart I love you?" I smiled. I did. I remembered him bringing me back to life in the living room. I remembered him teaching me fly-fishing in the Uintas, and our camping trips to Moab and visiting the southern Utah state parks. I remembered how much I'd liked being with him on the road in the Mack during that one summer; my first view of the sea off the Oregon coast was with him. He was remembering these things, too; we were sharing one synchronized memory, all the good parts we had together zipped past us. He chuckled and told me it was going to take him some time to learn to show love better, but I had to trust that it was true.

It occurred to me that I ought to cut him some slack. He'd only been dead ten years—that was only like yesterday here.

We got to a junction and had a few minutes. It reminded me of some type of railroad depot where a long track lay in both directions, neither of which end could be seen because they curved around a bend. Railroads in heaven shook my world almost as much as shrimp on the barbie did. What was this, my earthly way of thinking, or was Earth imagined from here? I thought of Plato's Forms. It seemed very natural for there to be this connection if consciousness was a continuous stream, but it was still hard to believe because I'd not been taught to think of the afterlife as mundane as this. I recall thinking these were symbolic impressions used for transmitting information through a human brain; I'd have had no bearings without familiar structure. I wanted to investigate this idea further to see if there was any physicality to the resemblance and as we were standing next to the tracks I observed how the rails had been laid by carving out a rocky shelf. I noted that they had dirt there. At least the notion of dirt.

I've always been drawn to the smaller details, but noticing dirt was more my way of handling the idea that these were my last few minutes with Dad. I understood the reason he and I were at a junction, and why the track ran out of sight either way.

Dad sensed our time ending too. I didn't know why he'd waited until the last minute, but it wasn't until then he brought up the Christmas room. The Christmas room brought up the wedding. He let me know he recognized culpability in my pain by wrapping his big arms around me; they were still cowboy arms, the arms I remembered. He still had his brushy moustache, and while I was pressed to his chest he told me that the Christmas room broke his heart. It was hard for him to witness my sorrow and hear every word couched in thought. He admitted that his leaving us for another family had changed the course of our lives and that his actions had had some unfortunate consequences, but he'd not realized how deeply his words had penetrated until I spoke my poison.

He asked for forgiveness, pleading his case in front of his one-person jury.

He stood justly accused but judged unfairly. We both knew that the hurt was unintended; privileged fifties-American-male ignorance was to blame, not his character. I didn't know if I bought it; selfishness is a character trait that culture only coaxes. He said I judged from a place of ignorance, I didn't know his whole story—it was not a brush-off, this time it was true. *There's things you don't understand, Jinnit Girl.* And then, as if this excuse held secret code, I did understand something; it was time to give up. It struck me that to judge him was to assume a moral superiority justified only by anger, and I wanted to judge so I could blame and feel righteous about it. This was a different deal than I thought it was. It was a matter of a child's expectations and a father's ability not matching up in the same lifetime that I'd made justification for my choice to be negative.

I knew all it would take to get my innocence back was to let go of my old way of thinking and simply trust as a child does that she's loved, but then my guide approached and, in a disappointingly practical way, Dad told me to run along and get on about my business. He had his own to do. It didn't feel like love, it felt like the same old disconnection.

I picked up the bag with the coat in it and began walking with the young man down the track. I didn't look back because I knew Dad wouldn't be there, that he'd gone back to the party and to people who accepted him, flaws and all. The track took us back to the white building where we'd started, only it was empty now and I could see that it was a theater. I was led up the grand stairs to the second-floor rotunda where there were many doors. My guide said I could choose any one of the doors. I could choose to see whichever movie I wanted. I wasn't really in the mood for a movie but I thought it was required, so I chose one. It was door number three. He opened the door for me, but stayed outside where he said he'd wait.

I took a seat smack-dab in the middle of the theater, and a man standing beside a screen on a stage briefly introduced me to what I was about to see. I watched a film. It seemed like God was narrating it. I don't remember much about it now though I felt it was deeply personal, meaningful only to me because I was the only one there. All the seats in this vast theater were empty. I remember thinking it was because it was a sunny Sunday afternoon and everyone was at the lake. When it was over I went outside and met back up with my guide. He told me things that seemed pertinent to me, so I was making a mental note to remember, but there was too much to keep straight in my head and I had a feeling I was going to have a certain amount of amnesia anyway.

I was feeling tired of being escorted around and told so many things. My head wasn't big enough to contain it all and I'd begun to lose interest. I was getting restless because I didn't belong here; I was anxious to be on my own. My guide knew this and our time together ended. I was glad because I'd been dying to try on the coat.

I somehow managed to find the secondhand store where I'd picked it up, which had a full-length looking glass. I took the precious leather out of the bag, elated at actually getting to wear it, when I was grieved to see the coat's age; it was not anywhere near new but very worn. It looked like it had been through a battle. I was overcome with sadness because I'd really loved this coat. In the short while I'd had it, I'd grown quite attached to it. I decided that I didn't care the shape it was in, I was determined to wear it, but once it was on me my sorrow was amplified when I noticed a disturbing hole on the left of my chest—it was a big tear right above the heart. I thought of disguising it but it was indelible, a fact of this coat. The thought crossed my mind that I could toss it and get a new one, but I just couldn't live with the idea. I'd just have to patch it.

I was trying to think of a nice-looking patch, when I was suddenly back in my bedroom.

The first thing I did was reorient myself. There were the bookcases that lined the wall, there was the dresser, and I was sitting up on the bed. I knew that just seconds before I'd been in another world because I not only felt it recede to the left of me, but watched as the light seemed to evaporate. It was a slow let-go of another real place. The physical sensations I remember having as I became conscious of the room weren't the usual upon waking up—I don't normally have to reorient myself to my own bedroom each morning, nor do I feel invigorated.

I rushed downstairs to share all this with David. I had to tell somebody about it to help me retain the memory while it was fresh. He was just starting dinner. He said it was something; he never had dreams like that—did I want rice or potato with the chicken? I was looking for a little more support so I called Judy, I knew *she'd* want to hear; she was always up for this type of amusement and she'd be the one to know if I'd been to heaven and back, because she'd know about Sheryl.

Meeting my older cousin on the other side was the only thing that could confirm or deny the reality of what had happened for me, because I honestly thought Sheryl was still alive. I'd certainly heard no differently. If she was dead then my visit was more than a dream impression; if she was still a grandmother in Ogden, then its reality could be discounted. Being two thousand miles away, Judy was my news source about relatives back home.

As soon as she answered the phone I asked, "Judy? Is our cousin Sheryl alive?"

"What? You mean Sheryl Parsons? Wade and Wiggy's sister?"

"Yeah Judy, the only Sheryl in the family."

"Why are you asking that?" It seemed weird to her. Weird to have me call out of the blue after months and begin the conversation about a cousin I barely knew. Since it seemed some kind of secret, I told her why. I told her that Sheryl sang for me as a validation and her laugh was as easy to identify. I related how she said she was here one day, gone the next—and then chuckled about it.

"Well that's something," Judy said, echoing David. "Because she did die, about a month, maybe six weeks ago. Geez, I was going to call you."

"I don't remember hearing about it. What happened?"

"Well it was a strange thing. She went to the dentist and had an allergic reaction or something. They said she went quick, I don't even think she made it to the hospital. I never made it to the funeral." Judy was stumped about what to think, but she was more interested now. "Hold on," she said. "Let me get a glass of wine and then I want you to tell me all about it again."

The demons raised in the Christmas room had yet to be put down before that Sunday over a decade later when I took an afternoon nap. Maybe it took me that long to process the resentment I could only allow myself to experience as disappointment, but it marked a turning point in my attitude toward my dad. It didn't happen miraculously: the Christmas room meltdown was the beginning of a lengthy healing process that involved taking the wind out of the grudge sails, and afterward, I still wished Dad and I hadn't missed the boat, but at least I wasn't dragging anchor. Telling me not to get my nose bent and to get it out of his business *was* love, I guess, because it probably spared me the rest of my life suffering to my own detriment. Forgiveness is letting go of a bad attachment. I wished I'd had the chance to get to know Dad better, but I could be free now to love the parts of him I got. Whether in the world's eyes he deserved it or not, it was enough to love him because I wanted to.

Since I couldn't remember the discussion with Dad and the men earlier, I assumed the purpose of this spiritual experience was a chance to settle these old scores. But whatever it was that Dad and I and the men spoke of privately, the thing I promised not to forget in one time zone—and not to remember in another—seemed to carry more gravity than Dad's setting me straight. I can't imagine why I'd have no memory of a promise I'd made. I can only hope that I will fulfill it.

As to the movie I watched behind door number three, it may have been this life review folks who've had near-death experiences speak about. Some might call it a projection from the Akashic record, the imprint of every thought we've ever had recorded in the Universe's energy field, the book the Bible has the angels writing in. I may have recently discovered significance with the number on the door. Though this experience happened many years ago, it was only recently that I came across a lecture on numerology. I didn't know until then that life paths had numbers, but I learned that mine was three. I don't know how much validity there is to this fringe science, but I do believe that math is God's language.

Allowing me to choose a door suggests that I chose this life path, and as it was a theater, I suppose I viewed its progress. I don't recall any grave upset afterward, but I do have memory of the man who'd hosted the review taking me aside and emphasizing something that I should either be aware of or expect. It wasn't cautionary, it was more like these folks kept repeating themselves, keen on pointing things out to me and focusing my awareness. I found it curious because it seemed to me that I already knew these things, or found them obvious, and I disagreed with being told things I was bound to forget.

This leaves me in summing up my thoughts on the experience with the embattled leather coat. Its symbolic link with the body *is* obvious: I put it into a bag when I arrived and slipped back into it upon departure. It looked like it had withstood about a half century of wear, but I still enjoyed it very much. I wanted being here better than there, and this coat was instrumental. Once I became aware I was carrying it, all I wanted to do was try it on. And even after I'd made the dramatic unwanted discovery that ruined the otherwise sturdy coat, I still chose to wear it rather than choose another. Did this choice I seemed to have in taking another body suggest reincarnation? Why else would there be this option?

This experience left me with many such questions because I was satisfied of its authenticity. Sheryl was proof that I'd witnessed truth, and I had testimony of a place that was similar to those who'd had near-death experiences, so I wasn't alone. One of my questions actually pertained to whether this had been a near-death experience—if I'd been faced with an actual choice to return to life that Sunday afternoon.

I'd considered what had happened to me as some sort of highly lucid dream or spontaneous out-of-body experience because the details were sharp and there were so many, but I hadn't considered it a near-death one until I reexamined the reason I lay down for a nap; I'd been having chest pain, indigestion I thought. But, having then been confronted with the tear in the leather placed as it was, I've wondered if it was more than heartburn that only mimicked a heart attack. I tried imagining it away the way I have sometimes done in lucid dreams, but it seemed inexorably a part of my mortality. Once I realized it was beyond my ability to fix, that it would be neither wished away or mended, a patch seemed the best I could do . . . for the time being.

Whether or not this patch was a figurative staunching-off of a real attack, I've always taken it to be premonition. Heart attacks are a common exit strategy for our family so there is reason to take it literally. Still, in light of our business, the healing words spoken between Dad and me at the junction, it may all be pure metaphor. The patch might not have been intended for a torn heart, but a couple of broken ones.

Nine

The Ghost Who Mimics

I've not heard the ceiling ghosts in ages, but Crookers hasn't exactly been at rest. There's been the sound of an eerily familiar imposter.

David the Second, who's been my companion for the last twelve years, is pivotal to understanding this particular ghost. Most of my adult life there's been a Janet and a David, just as the Ouija board had predicted. This David came into my life a couple of years after Jack; our kids were good friends and they hooked us up. Dave's a native Mainer, a laid-back union carpenter with a downeast accent and a good sense of humor.

Dave and I hit the road running, and soon he'd moved out to Pogey Point and in with me and the dogs. It was the first time since my divorce that I'd lived with anyone other than the girls. When the girls lived with me I didn't want anyone coming in and complicating our routine, especially after the Jack decade. But by the time Dave arrived, Jill had graduated from the University of Nevada Las Vegas and had moved from Vegas to Queens, and Amber was in Burlington in her senior year at the University of Vermont. For a while I'd been alone with Buff, my Golden retriever, and Zoe, a Shar-Pei mix.

At the time David moved in, I was teaching forty hours a week at an alternative high school program for pregnant teens and young mothers where we visited students in their homes. As I was on the road more than at the school situated in the next county, my home study served as my office. I was also working on a novel I'd begun after writing my dissertation so I spent a good deal of time in the study. In order to work on the book, I had to spend weekends, nights, and even some holidays tucked away in the tiny dormered, one-window room, where I was usually joined by Buff who monitored the hall and stairs, and Zoe snoring on the rug next to my Windsor.

This story begins on a Wednesday afternoon around three o'clock in my study. I'd had two cancellations and had gotten home from visiting students early, so I decided to work on the book until David got home. I had a good hour and a half. I was into it until about four, when I heard his pickup come up around the corner and pull into the drive. He was home a little early too. Buff barked once and then headed down the stairs with Zoe in tow, racing to be the first to the kitchen door.

I wasn't quite as excited as the dogs. I'd hoped to work a little longer. And it was garbage night. The chore had been put off for too long; one week he forgot to pick up garbage stickers and another week we forgot what day it was, so now the garbage had accumulated in the barn and was attracting skunks. It had to get put out that night. I heard Dave come in the front kitchen door and go out the back. I hollered down to him from the study window, reminding him it was Wednesday and to take out the trash. I didn't hear a reply, but it wasn't unusual not to get acknowledgment when reminding him of a chore. I heard him go into the barn and told him I'd be down in a minute to help. As I heard him beginning to separate the returnables that had stockpiled too, I reluctantly wrapped up and headed out to the barn.

I was surprised to find the barn door still latched when I got there, and that inside nothing had been touched. The bottles I'd heard rattling around still needed organizing, and the mucky trash the critters had carved up and spread was still waiting to be shoveled into healthier bags. Dave was nowhere around, certainly not there to help me. I figured he'd gone down to the vegetable garden as he sometimes liked to do when he first got home, and where he liked to go when there were unpleasant things like this to do. I called down to the corn patch but again got no answer, so I just went ahead and swept up the muck and relocated the black plastic stockpile from the barn out to the street myself.

That was when I noticed his truck was gone, and having been called early from my book to do this nasty chore myself, I felt twangs of building fury. I didn't want to go there, but I already had. I figured he'd gone up to the local Ma and Pa's, another place he liked to run off to, and the idea that he'd left this unpleasantness for me made me sour.

It was another forty minutes before Dave actually got home. I'd been giving him hell in my head all that time for no reason.

David hadn't been home earlier and he couldn't explain what had made me hear him when he wasn't there, but he admired its ability to get me to take on the barn singlehandedly; it'd been a real mess. He chuckled about how I'd had a right to be sour. I told him I didn't think he should take it so lightly, things like this could lead to trouble between us. Whether or not this was the aim, it was the beginning of what turned into regular pranking activity. Though it originated from various parts of the house, I only heard it from my study where I was usually deep in work and oblivious to the world at large. It might be that the silence of intense moments of concentration are good for listening on other levels. Anyway, this ghost was an impressionist and had David down to a tee.

It was common for Dave to come upstairs and check in with me when he got home. I looked forward to exchanging our days. He'd ask if I had some interesting traveling adventure on the county backroads on the way to see students, I'd get the general scoop on what his day had been like, then we'd discuss what we were having for dinner. I grew used to this household regrouping routine. It was a pleasant way to reconnect, until I started hearing David walk up the stairs and into the bedroom, cross the soundless carpet at the end of the bed, turn the corner with the squeaking floorboards, hear him leaning against the nursery threshold waiting for me to turn around, and then not find him there.

At first, I thought I was just hearing things, my mind jumping ahead to his arrival and our reunion, but I would sometimes falsely hear him come up the stairs on weekends in the middle of the day when I wasn't in an expectant frame of mind. This ruse continued once or twice a month for about a year, and as it felt harmless and I got tired of commenting on it, I mostly ignored it. I thought that refusing it attention was the best way of getting it to stop. But it didn't, probably because something like that can't be sufficiently ignored once the awareness is there.

One day it occurred to me that I always heard the sounds of someone walking up the stairs but never down. I put this together with the impression I sometimes had that I was being watched from the bedroom while working in the study. I'd been aware from time to time that I wasn't alone on at least some level, and I had the impression that the study threshold served as some sort of divide. On several occasions, after hearing the footsteps enter the bedroom, I'd gone to investigate, speaking to whoever might be there so I could figure out what the deal was. After a few times of this I felt like a pawn and refused to be bothered. When I heard the banister creak I'd just think, *Oh, here it goes again. Big deal.*

David quit coming up to regroup just to avoid confusing me. It was a loss in my day.

I told him I thought the house was haunted again; I reminded him about the whispers in the ceiling that had begun after we'd moved in and how I'd banished them, so while the girls were growing up there was hardly a peep. But it seemed now that the nest was empty the activity had returned. Dave passed the ghost idea off as a matter of convenience. What was he supposed to do about it? He was right, of course, what did I expect? Well moral support, at least—he wasn't the one sitting in the Windsor hearing ghostly approaches.

I decided to investigate further, take more of an offensive. I positioned the full-length mirror, which stood in a dormered corner of the bedroom, so that it captured the top few stairs, angling it so I had the advantage of seeing everything without having to get up and leave the room, by which time the activity usually dissipated. I didn't expect to catch an apparition, but it would have comforted me if I'd seen David the next time I heard the banister creak.

This ghost wasn't going to be caught with so little effort. In fact, now that it had drawn me to experiment, I was unwittingly encouraging it. Positioning the mirror only made it more creative, shifting its shenanigans to other parts of the house and shaking up the soundtrack. This convinced me we had a bona fide ghost rather than a residual stair climber, because tricking requires intelligence and planning.

After Buff died, it was up to Zoe alone to keep me company when I was working in my study. By then David and Zoe had become great friends. The sound of his pickup coming down the road and turning the corner was guaranteed to wake her out of a dead sleep. She always heard him before I did, cocking her head and, when certain, she'd tear down the stairs and be waiting at the kitchen door to greet him, whether he'd been gone all day or just five minutes. She wanted to continue the tradition she and Buff had shared, which was to celebrate his return by getting a good ear rub.

One day I was working on quarterly reports for the state from which the school received fifty percent of their operating budget. I hated doing quarterlies; they were time-consuming and no one really paid attention to them anyway. I was deep into Excel spreadsheets when Zoe suddenly perked up from sleep, giving me my first cue that something was afoot. She was off and running by the time I recognized the sound of the Dodge; sixty-eight pounds of fur flying down the stairs, thumping at the bottom, gaining traction again on the hardwood, turning down the hall, and finally arriving at the kitchen's French door breathless. It made me smile because I was glad Dave was back too. I needed a break from statistics and I needed some company. We were planning on grilling.

While I was wrapping things up at the computer, I heard him come up the porch steps—one is uneven and knocks if it isn't leveled. I heard the full-pane glass outer door open, then the French door to the kitchen that squeaked "welcome." I heard him sling his cooler-size lunchbox on the table and unpack it, set it out in the pantry behind the other door that squeaks, open the refrigerator, then run water in the sink.

"Hey," I called out as I went down the stairs. "I took a couple of ribeyes out." But there was no answer from the kitchen and when I got there Zoe was still waiting at the door. "Where is he, girl?" I asked, but the dog looked as perplexed as I did. I looked out the window and saw that the black pickup wasn't in the driveway. *Hmm, he must have gone back out for something, he does that sometimes, just gets here and leaves. He'll be back in a minute.*

But he wasn't. He didn't come home for another half hour; there was work being done on Route 1 in Winterport and he'd been stuck in traffic. I told him about hearing his arrival earlier. "Just hearing things again," he said.

I didn't know about that. *Zoe too?* "Why would we hear things that impersonate you? Why would we both hear you before you get here as if your own ghost precedes you home on these occasions?"

This ghostly imposter was always one step ahead of me and feeling pretty confident as time went on. Repositioning the mirror had somehow caused the activity to relocate to the bottom floor where it would just take more involvement to catch; all I had had to do when it occurred upstairs was to poke my head around a corner. Now I had to go all the way down to the kitchen to check. The impersonations grew so common that I began shouting out to Dave every time I heard a door open, and I became inordinately conscious of where he was in the house and what time it was. If it wasn't time for him to be home, then he wasn't. "Is that you?" I'd call out.

"Yeah, it's me, is that you?" I told him to stop teasing, I had to know what was up.

From then on the sounds spread to other parts of the house, but they always painted the same story. The sound of his pickup with the muffler going bad slowing on its approach to the house, the truck door thudding shut, the porch step rocking, and the kitchen doors opening and squeaking, the footfalls entering and exiting the pantry, or going outside to the back deck and coming in again. This entity had the movements of a man I knew and liked the sound of, down pat.

I was intrigued. Why would anyone find enjoyment in it? I mean, after a while the fun had to have worn off, along with my surprise. And who might this ghost be—and was it dangerous? I had no sense of any identity, but I tended to characterize its gender as a male for no reason other than it didn't seem like a female kind of tease. It was also impersonating a male. My only other experience with this sort of thing was with that fake one back in the Memphis apartment—he'd fooled me with the first-things-after-coming-home sounds of a husband too. Both happened to be named David; a coincidence, I felt.

I didn't see any connection between the men, but I was glad to have some comparison for refereeing the nature of the spirit. I ultimately decided that just as the Palmer and Crooker hauntings were two qualitatively different cases, these were two different beings employing similar tactics. The two cases were separated by some thirty-odd years, which meant if it was the same one I'd encountered in Memphis it would have had to have tempered its malice over that time. I didn't think it was possible. It hadn't given me the impression it wanted reforming.

I'd considered residual energy as I'd done when I'd heard the voices. Since these particular sounds had been made many times over and over, it was possible that I'd tapped into the imprint of David's evening routine trapped in the home energy field. Repetitive sounds may become strongly etched in a place over time, especially if backed by the power of a high point in one's day. A merry meet at the end of the day has much more energy than the morning's merry part; I was never troubled by hearing him leaving.

But a residual cause didn't fit. There was definite intelligence attached to these footsteps; it began one place and then relocated, and it could elaborate, build in a new sound or leave something out, and begin and end in different places. Sometimes this ghost David only got so far as the front door before he faded out, other times he got all the way to the bathroom and the shower. Whoever it was, they weren't falling for the mirror trick. Besides, old imprints left in the structural energy field probably couldn't account for hearing sounds peculiar to Dave, who'd been there for such a short time, or hearing them before they'd been made.

Nor could it explain the presence watching me through the nursery threshold.

I grew used to the more or less harmless activity, but I was always bothered by the deception. Deception is never harmless, is it? And then, once again what was the point? I finally decided to tell it, them, whatever was toying with me, to split. They'd been acknowledged, if that was what they wanted, and I'd been just curious enough to let them alone to do their thing and watch what developed. But it was getting old, and I didn't want the act evolving. By now I felt more comfortable giving my reasons for expulsion, expecting a reasonable ghost, and I encouraged them to go toward the light—or at least somewhere else.

The activity tapered off and soon ceased, but Zoe and I had gone down those stairs so many times and come up empty-handed that she took over Buff's old surveillance spot. She began sitting at the top of the stairs or halfway down them so she could see the driveway, making sure waking from a nap and the effort she spent on a greeting was worth it.

Ten

The Cottage in the Bottle

The young man dressed in white invited me to follow him into a forest, and after walking a short while the trees opened up into a meadow where there was a lovely little cottage at the forest's edge. It might have been modeled after one of those romantic ones Thomas Kincaid painted, straight off the English countryside. But we were not in England, we were at a place without a name.

I knew the cottage was Mother's simply because it looked like something she'd have liked. I've since read that in cases where an earthbound spirit is attached to a house, they seem much more amenable to the idea of crossing if told that they can recreate any house of their choice when they do. This choice in housing seemed to be true, because this was exactly the sort of thing Mom would have dreamt up. It didn't surprise me that it looked nothing like her beloved yellow brick house. Dad built our home in the fifties when the sprawling ranch style was in; I believe he designed it without much input from her because he was more contemporary than Mom in his tastes.

This place was designer humble, though Mom had afforded it many charming features. One of these was her garden. Being a gardener, too, I took notice of what she was growing and was surprised to find things like foxglove and delphinium, and delighted to see English ivy twining around a fence and wrapping the roof of the porch. These were plants she'd never been able to grow in Utah but always wished she could. I was thrilled for her. Here there were no climatic constraints.

She was standing under the roof of the porch waiting to greet me and there we exchanged hugs just as if it hadn't been the first time in nearly twenty years. She had her dark raven hair back and her youthful features, yet she didn't seem an age, just complete. I remember kissing her face; she seemed solid. It piqued my interest because I knew she was spirit. I reasoned that I was spirit, too, and that all spirit feels solid when in that form.

She welcomed me into the cottage, which I experienced as small; nonetheless, it was ordered and peaceful. I only have a sense of what its interior was like, nothing stands out clearly except, quite curiously, a wall sconce. The reason it probably does was because it surprised me to see such an ordinary thing. This preceded the family barbecue where ordinary would become a chronic surprise. Anyway, this sconce wasn't anything special, wrought iron with a tear-shaped bulb, but I kept glancing at it to make sure I was interpreting what I was seeing correctly because it just seemed to me to be the darndest thing. Mom noticed my repeated glances at the fixture and, apprehending my surprise, merely smiled.

I remember thinking she'd be glad I'd dropped in on her; I was thinking of all the things I wanted to say, the scoop I wanted to get. This was the place of answers. But Mom didn't seem prepared to answer questions, and wasn't as thrilled to see me as I'd expected. She didn't offer much hospitality, not even a place to sit. We stood briefly in the middle of one room before she said I had to leave, limiting me to only one of my hundreds of questions. I asked if she ever saw Grandma, and she said "all the time"; she saw a lot of her and Grandpa both. Ours would have to be a short visit; she'd just hoped to see me while I was there and let me know where she was. As I could see, she was happy and things were good, she kept quite busy. In fact she was right now engaged in an important project. It wasn't a place completely without care, but it was peaceful because there was plenty of time. Here there was time for everything.

Actually, that answered a lot of my questions.

Still, she told me I wasn't there to explore, I had come to see my father, and the guide was waiting to take me to him. I had the impression that she'd only piggybacked on Dad's visit, that the young man had granted her the favor of seeing me while I was in the neighborhood, but she must not take advantage of it. I said I didn't want to go, I'd rather stay with her. Why Dad? We didn't have much in common, he didn't even like me. She told me not to fuss, it wasn't up to her, and not to worry, either. She'd still be there when I came back, and now I knew where to find her.

I was disappointed, but she assured me it was necessary, so I went back outside to meet up with my guide. Mother waved to me from the porch then went back inside. I couldn't believe she'd just shoo me away as if she saw me every day. She was dead and I wasn't, so this was a rare opportunity. Then the ivy curling around the porch caught my eye and I fell again to marveling. I think it made such an impression because she'd dreamt up so much of it and, until then, I'd not realized how fond she was of something she'd never had. Still, I had slightly hurt feelings at my disposal. If there was time for everything why wasn't there time for me?

I remember asking my guide to explain Mother's cavalier dismissal, which he did, among other things, because we stood next to the garden for some time after Mother'd gone back in. I had the sense the reason behind her thrift had to do with this project she'd mentioned, that I was presenting a distraction to her, and that whatever she had going on involved a lot of study and focus but not me. It probably involved Grandma and Grandpa though, since she said she spent a lot of time with them.

In the years that I've pondered the nature of this project, I've come to wonder if it wasn't her next life's plan she was working on, the next act in her eternal progression staged with others in these soul groups that Dr. Michael Newton discusses in his book *Journey of Souls.* Based on his research into life between lives, the spirit world is described by thousands of individuals of all faiths and stations with amazing consistency while under deep hypnosis. I wonder if Mother was planning the weather for her next life and selecting an appropriate coat. From these accounts there is much to do in eternity: places to go, people to meet, and gardens to grow. It is not an idle world.

My guide explained to me how things were done. There were rules in the spirit world like there are physical laws here.

I remember being struck by how highly ordered things were—this seamless organization assured that nothing was missed, *everything* was accounted for. There really were Akashic records! A lot of people were involved too. There really were guides and councils. I remember knowing I was going to forget a lot of this so I made my companion repeat himself several times, thinking it would help my recall when I returned, but retaining this new knowledge seemed a little like Prometheus stealing fire from the gods. He told me I'd forget no matter what. Most of this I guess I did, because there are faint bits and pieces I'm aware of that let me know there was more to it.

I followed him away from Mother's cottage where we traveled, it seemed, through a field of tall grass that started out deep golden and quickly turned white. This bright patch we stepped through brought us out at the lake where I was left waiting at the picnic for Dad.

In recalling this experience I am left mostly with description. Little of the information I received through my guide came back with me, neither did an inkling of what the private meeting with the men and my father was about, or exactly what I saw in that theater. I was an inefficient Prometheus, and can only trust the fainter bits and pieces will be dispensed into consciousness on a need-to-know basis.

In writing this memoir I created such a need when I came to this jar. Mom and I were close so I was drawn to this mystery, the mystery of why it occurred, and especially why it occurred as it did. It was only very recently that I learned of Dr. Newton's work and became aware of the concept of soul plan projects, so I'd not valued the project Mom spoke of enough to explain her brevity. It just seemed odd to me that if Mother was that preoccupied with something else she'd have taken the time to see me at all, or she would at least have had better sense to pick a more convenient time. I *had* felt a bit of a bother dropping in on her like that, but I reasoned she must have been expecting me, or my guide wouldn't have taken the initiative to place me there. So, there had to be a good reason for it. I guess I was expecting something more dramatic than how she explained it; according to Mom she simply *wanted me to see where she was.*

But was that a good enough reason for a privileged astral visit? I'm sure many dead relatives would like to comfort their loved ones by inviting them to visit. It seemed somewhat unique. And why was this so important to her; more important than sitting down for a chat or a walk through her garden after twenty years?

It seemed so strange and out of character to me that I pressed on to find a reason, ultimately going back to a sequence of ominous dreams that Judy and I shared in the year after Mother's death. Mom might have been happily situated in a pretty little cottage, but these dreams suggested she hadn't gotten to her little slice of heaven right away. I interpreted them as meaning Mom had been bound to earth's astral sphere for a time after her death. What Judy and I touched upon here and there was how much these dreams could account for reality.

In Judy's dream she was standing at the kitchen window in Grandpa and Grandma Fluhman's old house, the very kitchen where three people died in the Ward tragedy. Judy had a baby on her hip, and ironically, so did the murdered mother at the time of her death. I don't know that one has anything to do with the other, but I think Judy was made for wearing babies. Out of her four, there are now nineteen grandchildren and six great-grandkids that have each taken a turn on her hip, and because I admire her, I like to brag how I was the first privileged one.

Judy saw Mom crossing through the orchard toward her and ran out to meet her. She was almost there when a man with a shovel jumped from behind our old boxelder tree in the backyard and separated them, scaring Mom the other way. It tore Judy up because she was sure Mom needed her help or was trying to tell her something. Mom had seemed desperate to get something across; neither this boundary nor her need to cross it seemed figurative—Judy just hoped the man with the shovel was.

Judy still swears it wasn't an ordinary dream because she doesn't normally have dreams where she wakes up screaming for her mother, and she hasn't had one like it since. Nor did she have any lingering upset with Mother's death that might have led to such a nightmare. Not until then had she begun to wonder where righteous, sweet-hearted women went. She'd always assumed they went straight to heaven, but she had a sinking feeling.

Around that same time, I had two similarly distressing dreams about Mom. Judy's dream was sandwiched between the first and last of them. In my first dream, I was underground, maybe in a basement. Mother's casket was there and I went over to it. She'd only been dead a couple of weeks and still looked the way I remembered her before the lid was closed. Except something was wrong, she was worried about something, and damn, it was just like her! She'd always been a worrywart, and I was disappointed at her unrest, surprised that she'd not escaped earthly concerns. What did that mean for me, or the rest of us, for that matter, if a sterling woman like her continued to suffer? She sat up in her casket to ask me something. She asked me *not* to do something—it seemed that I was the one who was keeping her there. Still, whatever it was she asked of me, I denied her; I refused to do what she wanted and I woke feeling terrible about it.

Awakening in an emotional state after this disappointing encounter, I quickly lost grasp of any other details, conveniently blocking out what I didn't want to see except for the feeling that her appeal had made me cross by putting me in a bad position. It left me with a sense of being at cross-purposes with my recently deceased and beloved Mother.

I was surprised that I'd have such a dream when I fully believed she was in a serene and peaceful place; in my eyes she should have been awarded some kind of medal for getting through life in one emotional piece and making it all the way to just sixty-eight. She ought to have been allotted a place where her worries were eliminated and her heart was completely satisfied. That was what I wanted for her, and I had complete faith in it, so for the subconscious to dredge up something so grim as bondage in a basement *was* surprising if not jarring. Along with this feeling that I was responsible for her suffering, the idea of there being an actual spiritual state like that caused me annoyance. I didn't feel guilty, but I felt like I should have for disappointing her real last request. I indicted myself for selfishness and felt crosser.

I chose not to pay any more attention to the dream to avoid feeding a bad idea, and because it occurred at a bad time. The kids and I were packing for Massachusetts then; I remember waking up and noticing the miserable furniture boxes stacked along the walls. I had my hands full preparing to make the two thousand mile trip with a three- and a seven-year-old, not to mention some apprehension of graduate school altogether. I had enough to worry about.

That should have been that. And it would have been, had this dream not been followed by a second, more disturbing rendition that made me wonder if the situation *was* authentic. I understood dreams to be a common avenue for spirit communication; it seems easier at the subconscious level where there's less resistance, but this dream felt more like astral projection because the details remained sufficient to leave an aftertaste of reality.

I was underground again in a crypt, or a place with long masonry tunnels that were dimly lit. Mother was there and we were standing at the edge of a wide beam of light that flowed in through a circular hole in the cave ceiling. I stood on one side of the beam, she stood on the other, separated by this light that was aligned with a stone well or some type of stone structure, maybe an altar. It had a meaning I couldn't grasp.

Mom asked me for help again and this time I was not feeling at odds with it. I just had no idea why she was asking me, either she was having trouble expressing herself or

I simply couldn't help. It didn't seem it was up to me anymore—whatever had been done was done. It seemed as if she had the freedom to leave this place on her own if she wanted. We argued a minute, not in anger but in understanding. She grew frustrated with me and gave up. This ended our chat and I began drifting upwards, lifted through a hole in the ceiling next to but not in the beam of light. I told her to come with me, it might cheer her up. I remember encouraging her to do this by assuring her it was alright; there were sparkles in the light that I sensed were others traveling the beam, so I knew it was safe and she wouldn't be alone. "Come on Mom, let's go," I coaxed her. While I didn't have much comprehension of what was happening, I told her not to worry and had complete confidence in this advice. But Mother recognized the ploy and hung back. She was surprisingly stubborn, which I think was the reason she was upset with me; there was something she was either afraid of or still waiting on.

I became aware that other beings were guiding my flight and I appealed for their help with Mother who I was fast losing sight of. I must have been traveling at a heady rate because she was suddenly at a great distance. But I could still hear her. She was warning me with some urgency to stay at the edge of the light, which I did. I traveled a moment or two in an upward manner until I was pulled away into the night.

After we arrived in Northampton and got settled, I called Judy to inform her of our situation and to tell her about the dream. In summary, I ended up pleading its case for reality. First off, it seemed strange, didn't it, that we'd both have dreams around the same time with such similarly disturbing impressions, especially when both of us felt at peace with Mother's passing? She and I, along with sister, Kay, had the responsibility of taking care of Mom in her last year. We'd had that time together to make peace with the inevitable, so it didn't seem a likely projection for two of the three daughters closest to Mom to have.

It wouldn't be for me, anyway; Mom and I had a solid farewell. On the day of her death she woke mysteriously out of a coma from which no one expected her to regain consciousness, and though I know folks do this sometimes, Mom's suddenly coming to life just hours before leaving it seemed a deliberate act to establish closure. I'd stayed with her the night before. I was in my final undergraduate semester at the time and in the morning I went in to tell her that I had to get to a final exam and was going to shower and get to class. I assured her Judy was coming to replace me, and told her I'd try and make it back that afternoon after checking on the girls, who were staying with a friend. Twenty minutes later when I returned to tell her goodbye, Mom's eyes were open and looking straight at me, clear as a bell.

I expressed my surprise and joy at seeing her again. Indeed, it felt like she'd died and returned. Only she was still broken; eighty-six pounds was all that was left of her. Her eyes didn't share my joy, only a sweet tiredness that communicated much between us. It was time to let go and we both knew it, knew she couldn't wait through the afternoon, that this was *that* moment, those goodbye moments we'd always known in our hearts we'd share one day. I'd been dreading them since I was a kid but knew they would happen, and now they were happening. I remember a helplessness at first, the hopelessness that followed, then the calm acceptance of our impotence to hold this back. The fear of the orphan was no less the sorrow of an adult daughter. I told her I loved her, and she mouthed this back. It seemed that was what she'd opened her eyes to tell me, and to let me know that she'd be on the other side that night.

For us it had been a good passing, so why would I conjure up something so atrocious?

Moreover, all three dreams countered our beliefs. Neither of us is religious but we share a spiritual nature, and both of us had confidence that Mom was in good hands. Yet Mom's failure to get her message across was heartbreaking. The man with the shovel was probably the metaphor Judy hoped he was, cipher for Mom's inability to communicate directly, her inability to influence us, or more pertinently, I felt, our inability to understand. Judy said she thought more concretely—that she'd always thought the guy was a grave digger, possibly a reminder to Mother that she was dead.

We laughed at the idea that someone wouldn't know they were dead and had to have someone like a grave digger tell them, but it was a bothersome compilation of subconscious images. We got a dark undertow when putting this menacing figure together with the cave where Mother was bound. It sounded like a pretty good version of hell. Judy protested Mom couldn't have been there, not if there was justice. If Mom wound up in anxious hell then we were all going. I just didn't see it as hell, either Catholic or Protestant, it was more like a state of expectant waiting, neither an aimless or indecisive limbo or stretch of personal torment, but a state of perpetual concern; a state one might associate with an earthbound spirit with loose ends.

Mother clearly had the option of taking the beam, so if this dream had any share in reality, she was putting it off for some reason and it wouldn't have surprised either of us if she had; she hadn't been ready to go and she might still have been a little upset about it. From the cancer diagnosis to her death, for two years she raged against the dying of the light, and maybe this prevented her from accepting it. Maybe those who had trouble passing had trouble crossing. At any rate, it probably hadn't come easy for her to stop worrying about her family. Whatever concerns she still had, it probably came down to this attachment.

Judy and I agreed that if souls chose to remain then Mom would have been a candidate, but the idea that she'd need help crossing felt uncomfortable to us. My dream certainly suggested this was what I was trying to get her to do, and Judy's dream also carried an unsuccessful boundary crossing. But it just sounded arrogant to think that a good woman like that would need characters like us encourage her to heaven. I believe all souls go when they're ready, that it's a personal thing others aren't fit to broker.

The best I could do was to pray for her, imagine her happy, and get on with my life. If Mom needed encouragement or release, prayer seemed the only avenue, but it just seemed insufficient. As Jill, Amber, and I were busy adjusting to a new community and routine, I didn't consciously attend to Mom very often; but when I did, I felt self-conscious, as if she was waiting on me to do something more than pray. Now she wanted me to act, not refrain. Whatever the nature of the burr was, I just couldn't be okay feeling that she wasn't okay.

It never occurred to me then but I do wonder now if this didn't have an impact on the way I came to feel about Massachusetts and the reason I wound up in Maine two and half years later. Though beautifully situated in the Berkshires with its quaint hill towns, the Pioneer Valley and I didn't click. A low-grade angst underwrote much of our time in Northampton. For the two and a half years we lived in Coolidge's Victorian, it was difficult to feel at home either there or on campus. Everything felt so temporary. I couldn't tell if it was just one of those energy disconnects I sometimes felt in upscale places, graduate school apprehensions, or if the dreams that preceded our journey—both their timing and haunting tenors—my tainted efforts to establish a relationship to the area with a pall of uneasiness.

All I know is that two and a half years hence I woke from a third dream with Mom in it, and after conferring with the morning from the window of a dead president, I was inspired to take that historical drive straight to the old Crooker homestead where the unsettling feeling I'd carried since her death finally dispersed.

The proposition that Mom chose to remain in what we call for lack of a better conceptualization an earthbound state of mind until her granddaughters and I were settled, isn't as much of a stretch as some might think. I can strengthen the case by several factors if I include Mom's personality and her value system, my situation, and the timing of things. Spiritual experiences are very personal in nature, and highly situational. What I've proposed so far is a result that remains inconclusive until fair probable cause is added.

I was newly divorced at the time Mom got sick. The girls and I had been on our own for only a short while and she worried about us constantly, especially as a move from our luxury mountain home to a tiny two-bedroom apartment was a worrisome step down in circumstance to her. I did my best to assure her we were happy getting by, but she wouldn't have it, having had the experience of single parenthood herself.

When I told her of our plans to move East she'd been truly aggravated with me. I was the only one of the six of us without a spouse at the time, and this seemed too risky to do all alone. I could tell she was already imagining horrors like breaking down on the freeway, complications with the U-Haul, and trouble finding a place when we got there. There was probably a rapist waiting along the way. Basically it meant a separation of the flock she felt more comfortable having all together and she asked me *not to go*. I didn't tell her I wouldn't because she knew I would, but she let me know she very much *wished* I wouldn't; her frustration with me was *very* well communicated through the look she gave me.

It makes sense that this could have all played out again a few weeks after her death as a guilt-tripping dream. It was the last thing she asked of me and I denied her. But what makes the scenario involving a mother's ghostly re-appeal more likely to me was the thoughtless timing of this news.

It was a big mistake in the first place to tell her of plans I assumed she'd want to know about, to assume that a doctorate would relieve her fears for our welfare rather than upset the apple cart. I thought that to her education was a symbol of success that trumped relocating risks. Even though I was well intended, it was a stupid assumption. Unfortunately, the timing of the news was far more stupid—I told her this just after receiving the acceptance letter, when I was newly excited to share my news with her the way we had always shared things together. I guess I really didn't realize she was on her actual deathbed; maybe this was a way of refuting it, by returning things to normal, but a month or so later she slipped into that final coma.

Anyone who knew her would know that news like this delivered at death's doorstep was enough to keep her. The thought of me and her two little granddaughters traipsing two thousand miles away from the flock was enough to have a mother like mine reappearing in dreams, and when this failed, appealing to the only sibling who had any influence on me. Maybe I was the child on Judy's hip in the dream. I thought about how Mom had come back on my watch her last day, and making the connection with my blunder, I was forced to reappraise our last passing moments. Had this worrisome business still between us—aggravated by my leaving that morning, her leaving that night—driven her struggle to consciousness? Could there have been a last appeal for a change of mind in her sweet, tired eyes?

The thought kills me, but it fits that I was the one keeping her in this unsettled state by delivering my good news, for her to worry over, just on the brink of giving up the ghost. If I'd refused to stay put then she'd have to until we'd found ourselves a place—something unrealistic for us in the swanky Berkshires, but doable on a remote point of land just shy of Canada.

Location seemed to be important to my mother. I guess because it established welfare. She let me know the day she died that later that night she'd be on the other side, then through dreams she informed me of her earthbound state or earthbound state of mind in spiritual territory, so I'd be open to her nudge toward Pogey Point, and she could finally get to her cottage betwixt wood and meadow. Twenty years on she invited me for a visit, or at least took advantage of one so she could show me where she was, and I think it was to rest any lingering doubts about her welfare these dreams had roused.

Then it was pretty much back to business.

Mother's expediency, which so troubled me, would make sense if it was related to the time it took to soothe my mind; it wasn't that we didn't have more time, time was currency there and there was an eternity of it. We simply got whatever time it took. Ordered places run practically. It also shed light on my complaint of lack of affection. My guide mildly rebuked me for taking personally law and order—my notion of thrift sprang from ignorance about the way things were done, but my annoyance with Mother's demeanor came from misunderstanding the soul's faceted nature.

My annoyance was that I'd taken in more of her garden than I had of her, and notwithstanding the "project," her thrift with me was perplexing because it was so unlike her not to want to reconnect. She seemed more sedate than I'd known her to be, not completely the mother I was familiar with. Did people really change that much in the spirit? Did some of them just stop being who they were?

My guide answered by pointing out how sometimes life only allowed for the expression of a few aspects a soul had. This wasn't fated, it had more to do with the way we chose to respond to life, what muscles we used, sometimes the exertion of certain ones came to define us in exclusion to others. The reason Mother didn't seem like the mother I'd known was because she wasn't there. Earthly vicissitude had never allowed me to know her as serene and peaceful, but this was who she was capable of being.

I always begin my writing day soliciting inspiration from the Universe, gambling on my thoughts and trusting spirit to let me know when I've hit the jackpot. I usually know when I have because the answer is so satisfyingly apparent. This is how it felt to me when things started rolling into place. For me, connecting these dots was like recovering parts of the conversation I had with my guide standing next to Mother's garden fence.

Eleven

Ghosts that Tickle

This chapter covers ghosts who tickle hair, ribs, and sometimes your fancy.

Somewhere in time my favorite brown leather rocker that sits in front of the hearth became known as the captain's chair. This chair sits in a room we remodeled a few years ago—what would have been a back parlor at one time, the front one being the Christmas room.

When we remodeled, we put in a new chimney, then dismantled the brick fireplace and replaced it with stone. David and I had fun scouting for rocks with personality to face it with; I knew I'd be sitting there a long time looking at it and I wanted it to be aesthetic as well as energy compatible. We sought for stones in the places we loved most, like the woods up at his camp or the beach down the street.

When it came time to select from the pyramid on the driveway, I chose according to texture, grains, and colors, and for the memory it held of the time and place we found it. Some have secret meanings we hold between ourselves.

One night I was sitting in the captain's chair watching the BBC news with David, who sat opposite me in a burgundy recliner. I felt something moving in my hair. A spider, I thought—once in a while one will drop down from the exposed beams. I ran my fingers through my scalp and tried to shake it out, then dusted off my arms and shoulders. A few minutes later, I felt it moving again. I thought I must not have gotten it. I stood up and shook myself off. David told me to stop acting weird, I was interrupting the BBC. The next time it happened, a minute or two later, I swatted at the air trying to take down the invisible web. I finally went for the duster, not resting until I'd done the whole room and the news was over.

This may seem a rather bold declarative statement, but I've since come to think that what I could only account for by way of a spider then were ethereal fingers stroking my hair. It hadn't been the first time my hair had been stroked by a ghost, the salon owner I ran into at the orange juice case started it. When this began I hadn't known hair touching was a somewhat common thing for ghosts to do, cither out of curiosity or in affection, but many female complainants and paranormal investigators had experienced it. Learning this, I decided to test this new impression. If it happened again I would wait to react, give myself the time to distinguish what it was before imposing a nature upon it. Sitting still and dismissing spiders the next time I felt this tickling of my scalp and sensed movement, it actually did come closer to the sensation of stroked hair better than a surface-traveling spider. I got up and brushed myself off though, just in case.

I spend a lot of time in this area of the house; it's my center of gravity. Before I quit teaching to write full time, I bought myself a laptop, which freed me from my study upstairs; over the years the Windsor's gotten harder and I've enjoyed my isolation less. Now I write in the captain's chair beside the stone hearth, which is usually lit for warmth and company. I think it's this nexus between neurons, the chemical fire and the fireplace's stone face, along with half a dozen green plants in clay pots and the ceiling's old beams, that accounts for this room's pleasant energy and serves as a spirit attractant. Combined with respirating foliage and water trickling below us, all the elements for magic are here. Maybe it's simpler than chemistry and physics—maybe this place attracts spirits who just like cozy homes.

I wouldn't say the parlor's more haunted than any other room, really. When compared to my bedroom and study, the kitchen, and especially the pantry, it isn't. It's just that there's a floor lamp positioned over my shoulder on one side of the captain's chair, and on the other there's often *something else.*

This area will often attract Zoe's sudden interest from where she's lying on her bed at the foot of a bookcase across the room. Sometimes she'll stare into the air upwards to the ceiling, just to the right and a little behind me, then her eyes begin circumnavigating the room as if watching somebody walk around us. Sometimes she'll get up to inspect, tracing something along the floor and giving the hardwoods a good sniff test. At first I defaulted to spiders. It could have been one that came down on a web to the floor; the old farmhouse seems blessed with them. But after I'd begun to observe more carefully, I never found a spider, ant, cricket, or fly that would explain Zoe's interest and actions. I was thinking this dog was seeing something or this dog was weird. Dave thinks weird is bred into Shar-peis, but I know they were bred to be loyal guard dogs for the emperors of China. Was Zoe seeing the ghost who was stroking my hair? Could it have been the angel in the grocery who planted this hair stroking as some recognizable sign?

While this activity began around the captain's chair, it wasn't confined to it.

One night I was reading in bed and felt the stroking again. It definitely wasn't spiders unless there were five of them all traveling the same direction. I put down the book and closed my eyes, wanting to fully experience it so I could decide who it might be. I'd feel better if it was someone I knew, like Mom or Grandma, or the grocery ghost, but it might not be. I lay still and tried to determine if I liked it: it was a sort of litmus test for measuring ghostly intention. I figured if it was a pleasant interaction and didn't scare me then it was a good ghost. If it was unpleasant or annoying, then it was not such a good ghost to have around. What I felt was definite stroking, a soothing sort of motion; comforting like what a parent would do for a child. It wasn't meant to scare me; someone simply wanted me to know they were nearby and could affect the physical world in these small ways.

This would occur off and on for about a month when I was stationary, either writing or while in bed. Once I felt it while standing at the sink doing dishes. Then it stopped. I didn't know if I was wrong about this ghost, if it only started out innocent then transformed, or if it was another one completely, but around the time the hair stroking stopped something began truly upsetting the dog.

I've got a reputation for having a green thumb. Apart from the gardens outside, I have several indoors. David calls it a jungle as every radiator beneath a window supports something green in a clay pot. During the winter I experiment with bulbs, forcing paperwhites and hyacinth to help dress up a dreary February or March day. I also have a few hard-to-grow varieties I'm particularly proud of. Among them is a zebra plant that's grown to five feet—a gorgeous specimen for not being in a greenhouse or the Amazon. I enjoy my green thumb so much that I began documenting my gardens in photographs. Every so often when some variety did something awesome, I'd take its picture, and maybe Zoe, too, if she was handy.

Several months ago I was taking pictures of twelve bright yellow blooms on the green- and-white-striped zebra plant.

I became aware that Zoe was acting peculiar. She insisted on standing right in my way, standing where I wanted to stand, as near to me as physically possible. I budged her a time or two, but she'd scoot over all of a whole eighth of an inch. At first I just thought she was being stubborn and holding her ground, but then it occurred to me how unlike her that was. You'd have thought she'd turned to granite. The other odd thing was where her attention was riveted; she was staring at the glass door in the kitchen. I couldn't see anything behind it, so I waited to see if I could hear anything, like maybe an animal snooping around outside.

"Come on girl, move your butt," I told her with some persuasion from my knee, "I need to get the zebra from the other side." With my nudge she crept onto the black- and white-tiled squares that mark the kitchen, slowly made it across to the chopping block, past the stove, and to the French door that was closed to the narrow corridor on the other side. This place was her traditional greeting spot, the place she went to when she heard someone coming, but she wasn't excited—she was more expectant, a bit leery and defensive, she lowered her head as if preparing an attack.

I waited to see if she was going to decide she wanted water; her bowl was on a braided rug nearby. She wasn't interested in water, she was intently studying the foyer that led to the front door. I went and looked out—there was only a chair, a wreath, and a basket in it. Since I had the camera in hand I snapped a picture; all I got was glass reflection but it seemed to snap the dog out of it. She stopped at the water bowl on her way back to her bed. I went back and finished the photo shoot with the zebra.

I might not have worried about this episode had Zoe not already been acting weird, and if I hadn't felt that the activity in the home was changing into something of concern. Zoe was definitely on guard, and this had me nervous about what she was seeing on the other side of the door because it began happening frequently, every other night or so. The only time Zoe was interested in the door was when she was waiting for someone to come through it, and by her reaction she was either expecting somebody who didn't show up, or watching somebody who'd already arrived. I figured if it was scaring her then it should be scaring me, which made me feel less silly about it.

Then a week later something woke her out of a dead sleep. She's an old dog of thirteen years so she doesn't usually spring up like that, but she did, like some warning bell had been set off and she was still a puppy. Following her instincts I went into investigation mode. Zoe hesitated as usual before entering the kitchen, waiting where the checkerboard begins and the hardwood ends, her attention this time riveted diagonally through the threshold that leads from the kitchen to the pantry. This was the matching French door opposite from the one she was usually drawn to. "What are you seeing, girl?" I asked her, worried she might be looking beyond the room through the screen door that opens to the back deck. Was someone out there? Maybe whoever had been stopped at the front door was trying the back. I went and got my pepper spray.

By then Zoe had crept all the way to the door. Her muscles were tense, I reached down to stroke her and could feel her neck and shoulders vibrating. I wondered if this was fear or predatory instinct, if she was sensing something odd or something dangerous, whether it was a human intruder or nocturnal wildlife. I imagined a skunk or raccoon was trying to get into the barn, but then why didn't she bark? I put on the porch light and stepped outside to take a look around, making as much racket as possible to scare whatever it was away. Zoe came to the door and looked out when I returned to trade the pepper spray for the camera. I fired off shots around the kitchen, pantry, and parlor, and even ventured outside and pointed at the back deck in the dark. I didn't know what I expected to catch, but reviewing the pictures I found nothing out of the ordinary.

About two months passed before I uploaded the zebra photos. I forgot about them until the next day when I was finishing up writing and about to shut the computer down, when something told me to go back and look at the photos. So I did. Something caught my eye in the one I took of the hearth and captain's chair, when I was halfway hoping to catch my hair-stroking ghost or whatever Zoe found so interesting. In that picture I saw one large transparent orb to the left and a little behind the chair.

I didn't know if it was the hair-stroking ghost, but it tickled me because it was my first orb. I'd never known what to think about orbs, so I basically discounted them the way other skeptics do—as dust or moisture particles. This orb was near the fireplace and couldn't have been moisture, and I found the idea—that it was one solitary gigantic transparent dust particle that, taking into account the space it took up on the hutch's panel it appeared in front of, measured about eight inches across, and just happened to be in the spot as my suspected ghost—a little bit of a stretch. Viewing the orb magnified, I saw it was filled with intricate and colorful patterns, and I could see a corona or aura that surrounded it; it looked like the electromagnetic field around all living things. This thing looked alive to me, and I couldn't discount its interesting location, but I had no way of knowing if it was sentient.

As I went on to review the rest of the photos I found other orbs. I showed them to David, who doesn't generally believe in things he can't see. "Well you can see that, can't you?" I pointed out the solitary orb behind the captain's chair, "And look there's others, some brighter, some in *your* chair." David was really interested now, he'd endured enough paranormal programming to know orbs were suspected spirits, and my little Kodak suddenly assumed a new career. We went orb hunting, and like the voices saying "they're here" from the television screen in *Poltergeist*, or the way they had from my bedroom ceiling, we uncovered proof the orbs were everywhere—proof that things like this existed that have never been sufficiently explained. Until proven otherwise this was possible proof of spirit expressing in the physical dimension.

What are these see-through circles containing prismatic colors? I wouldn't call them bubbles because they only appear two dimensional, round and flat, more like discs, though this may be a photographic artifact. Magnified, differences can be seen. The electromagnetic field surrounds some imperfectly, and all are constituted a little differently. Like snowflakes or people, they have varying degrees of intricacy, opacity, and brightness. They don't behave like dust particles do, they seem to come and go at whim, not ever simply drifting but moving in all directions. Unless there was a strong air current, dust wouldn't move like that; a columnar blur as it passes through space wouldn't be photographed at a diagonal. I've seldom caught one in the same spot even if there was only a fraction of a second's difference between two shots. And with dust there are usually communities, not single particles; dust travels in microscopic clouds.

Finally, if they are just atmospheric particles, why do they seem to hang where I'm at? If we have spider webs then we've got dust, but how come this "dust" seems so sociable, hanging around our chairs instead of the rug or the ceiling? And why now? Why am I finding them *now*?

I went back and looked at other pictures I'd taken of the outside gardens and the ones inside that I'd taken earlier, but found them all clear. Was it the camera? No, because since we'd been shooting for orbs, plenty of places in the house had come up clear. The outside shots, particularly around the spruces, are amazing examples of this mysterious phenomenon; whatever these energy bundles are they seem to like the trees as much as the doves do. But while the doves come home every night to roost, these things the camera caught are not always there.

I've tried documenting this activity by date and time, to see if I can find correlations with the planetary energy fluctuations having to do with phases of the moon. There seemed to be a flurry of orb activity around midmonth in February, just days prior to a new moon, and in the weeks following as the moon waxed, the activity dwindled to nothing. If there was any association, it was the opposite of what I'd expected. It's generally believed that energy waxes as the moon does, and wanes along with it. If there was any correlation between spirit activity and moon phase it was converse to lore; in March, around the same time of lunar darkness, activity picked up again. Except this time, I was able to catch more than orbs; I encountered something quite spectacular. Spectacular because before when I'd seen photos like this, I'd not have believed them.

We'd had a mild spring. In Maine we don't regularly get sixties and seventies in March, but we'd just had a comfortably warm sunny week with low humidity. It was just after midnight and I had the back porch door off the pantry open to let in the crisp, fresh air. I often stand at this door and look up at the stars; a rural sky provides the best canopy, and from there I have an unimpeded view of the Milky Way running over the back of the house and the Big Dipper arching above the chimney. This was one of those clear, completely calm and starry nights when I might drag the old telescope out. Anyway, there was no significant weather to account for what turned up in my photo.

I'd just begun documenting orb activity, and on this night I had the notion to take photos off the back deck where we'd seen orbs in the spruces. I'd taken shots on a regular basis whether I found anything or not, and just as things had been going the past several weeks I didn't expect to find anything. It seemed a dry spell in the cycle of activity. I checked the first few pictures I'd taken and they all came out clear, so I decided to switch strategy. I left the rail and returned to my stargazing doorway, stepping up into the pantry and taking a panoramic succession of shots from the threshold of the house.

I began at one corner of the deck closest to the house, sweeping left to right around to the other corner where it connected with the barn. *Click*; I circled slightly. *Click*, the flash lit up the white railing against the darkness. The next lit up the trees, and the next one, taken about center and right in front of me, caught a white form that floated above the deck. It took up a good amount of space and was right in my face. Indeed, at that instant I saw it, that was what came through—I was *face to face*. Considering that I'm five-eight and the pantry door was elevated above the deck a good ten inches, this meant that it floated about seven feet in the air. The next shot was shifted to the right only a speck and taken a split second later, but this mass was gone.

I knew I'd caught something so I hastily reviewed the images. Nothing, nothing, *this thing*, nothing. It manifested extremely fast, whatever it was. I noted conditions in my tablet, sixty-eight degrees—too warm to mistake it for breath—no measurable wind, no moisture, no bad camera. When the photo was printed off and viewed at different angles, it looked like an Egyptian cat goddess to me, one of those thin statue-like cats that usually depict Bastet, the protector of women. To everyone else, like Amber, David, or our neighbor Kristen, it looked like a winged creature with horns that I saw as cat ears. They were sure they detected winged appendages and they were all in agreement that it was related more to devils than angels. I was intrigued. All of them are skeptics so I had expected more caution from them in declaring it a demon.

Maybe they are more sensitive to the situation than I because I feel completely neutral about it. For now it was just an unexplained phenomenon that I can't assign morality, though its color does comfort me a little since it isn't one of those nasty black-shadow people that folks often report. I'd like to think it does represent protection, but for now it's just a shape in the weather—a photo of an instant cloud that came and went in the blink of an eye.

In April, May, and June, during the months of spring associated with rising energy, we caught very little activity.

I was a little disappointed when the pictures turned out clear because these orbs were a mystery that tickled me. I was also hopeful of photographing the white form again as an apparition is more credible than orbs; firmer evidence of the other side. David concluded it had to be the camera, though would a defective camera be defective only some of the time, only at certain times of certain months? Only on certain pictures?

Then, in July, I saw a similar white anomaly again, another roguish cloud, and this time I had a witness but was without the camera. The unusually warm temps we'd been having since early spring constituted a trend that carried on into summer, and by June we'd worked up to regular daytime temps in the mid and high nineties. Being on the coast these temps created a good deal of humidity and we had our share of thunderstorms. Then in July the weather stabilized and became unusually pleasant. The daytime temps normalized to around eighty, the nights to a comfortable seventy, and I took advantage of the warm, arid evenings for walking Pogey Point with Zoe.

It was a late July night around ten-thirty and we were out under the light of a full moon. I prefer walking the dog at night because she's unfriendly toward other dogs and it lessens the chance we'll have conflict. I also like being out in the world when I can have it more to myself. We had just turned off from the main road onto Petticoat Lane—this is a short side street that runs alongside my property and dead ends at a grass field, which in July is about four feet high.

We'd walked only about thirty feet down the lane when I was startled by a discrete white mass drifting over the field straight ahead of us, going from right to left. From my distance of around a hundred and fifty feet, it looked formless but had the height of a tall human and just less the same width. From where I stood, in utter surprise, it appeared to be a five-by-six cloud. It traveled very quickly and moved in such a smooth, unhindered motion that I dismissed it as human or animal because there was no gait. And it was too high above the ground. It literally drifted at a constant rate under its own power over the field of four-foot-tall grass. Zoe saw it the same time I did and tried taking off toward it, agitated by my pulling back on the lead and leading her in the other direction.

I suppose if I'd been a serious investigator I'd have followed it. But I was spooked. Of the thousands of times Zoe and I had walked Pogey Point in the dark, we'd never caught a ghost walking its fields—at least not one that we could see. While I felt privileged to have been present to witness it, my intuition told me to let it be. Letting this soul enjoy this private pleasure was the right thing to do.

I was up late one night reading in bed. Dave was snoring beside me. I finally decided to turn out the light and get some sleep. As I was falling away I had that vague sense that someone was stroking my head again. I went to sleep with a smile on my face. Not long afterward I was aware of two personages standing at the bedside, a man and a woman. This was a space between the bed and a bookcase with a table heaped with books in between. I remember my first thought was how two people had managed to fit themselves into the small space. Two people couldn't do it. Then I noticed that they didn't fit very well, one was standing slightly behind the other. The reason this was important to me was because it meant they were taking up physical space, relating to it. I didn't know who these visitors were, only that they were ghosts and they were not bothering to scare me, so I trusted myself to go with the flow and waited for them to let me know why they were there.

They had a short consultation with one another, as if to agree on the way to proceed, then they reached down and touched me. The woman was behind the man and was more timid about it. I was startled that they had some kind of density I could register. I definitely felt fingers, like the fingers in my hair, only these were tickling me in the ribs of my right side. I assumed they were playing but I was too worried to laugh; it was an odd thing for a ghost to do, wasn't it? I was feeling slightly embarrassed and about to fend them off when pressure was applied and their fingers dug more seriously into my flesh. It sent a strange cold sensation rippling through my side and into my chest. It was like some kind of electric shock. I was squirming to get away and David was starting to wake up.

Good. I wanted him to see these ghosts, and I wanted *him* to tell them to go. Maybe they would then. "What's the matter, hon?" he asked, half-awake.

"*Ghosts*," I whispered and pointed to where they were standing, but they didn't stay long enough for him to get a grip. I told him about the tickling. He said it was the "damndest thing" before falling right back to sleep. I lay there trying to fathom why spirits would bother to tickle anyone.

I bought an EMF detector after this. I had the notion of putting it in the bedroom during the night, but I couldn't find a way to keep the gauss meter's button on for longer than a few minutes. I found it interesting to see where the areas of highest radiation were in the house, but it seemed to be the meter's only advantage. One night I wanted to have a little fun, so I took down the gauss meter, dusted it off, and started measuring the field around the captain's chair. "Be ready," I told David.

"What?"

"With the camera. Have it ready if this thing suddenly goes off."

He wondered why he put up with me.

I sat down in the rocker and with my right hand I swept the meter a hundred and eighty degrees around where I was sitting. The left side of the chair where we'd discovered the first orb took a hit. The meter hissed noisily. "*Now, David*!" Oh my God, he was dozing through this. "Hey you, wake up, come on, take a picture." He snapped one off.

On the review we found one solitary, perfectly shaped orb two feet above my head. Just about where the head would be if a person was standing behind me. The orbs were back. The one thing that occurred to me was that it was again mid month, near the time of a new moon.

I went in for my routine yearly physical. The female doctor, about the same age as I am, was checking my breasts, checking the record to see when my next mammogram was due. She raised my arm and ran her hand down my ribs, where she stopped and brought out a magnifying glass. "This has got to go," she said, laying the glass on the metal tray and handing me a mirror.

I looked at what she was referring to. A mole with a raised jagged edge.

"You haven't noticed it?" she asked, surprised.

"Sure, but I didn't think it was anything. I've had it a while." I asked if it was cancerous. She said she couldn't know for sure without a biopsy, but looking at it, it was best to go.

"Lie back down," she instructed me. "I can take that off right now. Shouldn't hurt too much, just feel a pinch." She excised it, and we ended by discussing hormone replacement therapy to help with the hot flashes. She suggested wild yam root from the co-op.

When David got home I told him about my operation, lifted up my blouse, and showed him where the surgery was. It wasn't until then we realized together that Dr. Kramer had just taken off the tickle spot.

"Do you think they tried to warn me?" I asked him. He didn't know what to think.

Having a hazardous mole removed from the very spot where the tickling had turned to pain didn't verify a visitation. I knew it might be a mind-body phenomenon. My body sensed something wasn't right and told my subconscious about it. These "ghosts" could have been the brain's way of getting the message across.

Either way, it's still pretty cool.

Twelve

The Pantry Ghost

Our pantry is immediately off the kitchen. We have to go through it to get out to the back deck and the barn that attaches to it. Another door leads down to the cellar. It was originally used as a mud room and later became the laundry. A few years ago Dave and I decided to remodel, opening up the small space by putting an antique arched window into the southern wall and replacing the original solid-core four-paneled door with a modern glass, French style. The floor shares the kitchen's new black and white chessboard tiles and maple wainscoted walls.

To allow the washer and dryer to fit into a snug alcove, we expanded one wall by shortening a set of steps that ran to the cellar. This allowed us another three feet, but it eliminated a quarter of stair width, and along with it, some shelving that was once used for fruit storage. When I got here many of the old Mason jars, loose lids, and rings were still here, too, and I sort of regarded it as a personal touch that confirmed this was the place I ought to be. I hated dismantling the shelving, but it was the only way we could squeeze both appliances into the same space.

It's a small room that took on a big mystery almost as soon as we'd finished remodeling, and it had the signature of another prankster ghost. I couldn't tell by the nature of things whether the David impersonator I've told to go had returned, or a new, more technologically advanced ghost had arrived—all I knew was that there was a short hiatus in activity and when it resumed the spirit had a fascination with the washing machine.

At first it was just a small matter. I would hear the washer button being set while I was in the kitchen or parlor; it was the beep of the electronic signal that warns a new cycle is about to begin. I thought it curious when I hadn't put in a load. I got up and went to turn it off. Maybe we had electrical problems with the Whirlpool. A while later I heard it again. I turned the pantry corner and there it was, the green light blinking.

This continued intermittently for weeks, but David couldn't find a reason for it.

One night I let Zoe out. I opened the back door to the deck, hooked her up to the run, stood there and watched as she traipsed down the steps that led to the lawn. I shut the door and as I was leaving the pantry, the washer light beeped and came on. *Stop horsin' around*, I thought, just in case there was an unseen practical joker in the room with me. I always start out with good-natured humor when I'm communicating with someone I don't know. It works like a charm to neutralize the situation. I pushed the button back off, and returned to bring Zoe in about fifteen minutes later. I unhooked her, patted her on the rump, and she headed to the bone jar. I shut the door and as I was turning around I noticed the dryer door was wide open, the light was on, and the drum was empty. "Okay, really stop it," I said out loud. "You're starting to scare me a little and friendly ghosts don't scare." I was wondering why if a ghost had something to say, they didn't just say it.

In examining the situation I've come up with two things that may be related to the activity. The first was the remodeling we'd done; it wasn't anything major but I'd heard how even small alterations in an old house could sometimes stir things up. The other thing had to do with the sod cellar mentioned earlier that bears describing now. The house's stone foundation and earth floor makes for a dank, unpleasant place; it's like Mother's fruit room writ large. The asbestos still drips from the pipe-lined joists in white wisps, so we have to hunch over when walking through it to escape contact, and the whole place is meagerly lit by two light bulbs that dangle from the old knob- and tube-wiring. Like the old fruit room, the earthen corners are unlit. It was used as a root and fruit cellar back in the day, but its only modern use is to house the furnace and oil tank.

As I mentioned earlier, during spring a small river runs beneath the house along the dirt floor of the cellar. This ditch was planned by Crooker as drainage, but unfamiliar with this old-fashioned engineering I thought my basement had flooded the first time I saw it. The water runs underneath the parlor and drains beneath the pantry area. That's why I think this feature may be related to the pantry activity. Now I wondered if the Whirlpool's problem stemmed from the remodeling we'd done combined with this unusual electromagnetic feature.

One summer day I was standing next to the washer where I'd placed a wrought iron sorting table. At least it was meant for that purpose originally, but now it stored an assortment of vases. I was looking for a vase for some white lilies I'd just cut. The green light on the washer went on. I was hardly a foot away from it and couldn't help feeling this was personal. It was either an electrical circuit with a mind of its own, or something wanted me to know it was there. I paused to assess the situation. It felt like more than a glitch in the wiring to me—there seemed to be deliberate intention behind it; something seemed to be challenging me for acceptance.

I told Dave the Whirlpool's problem might be related to the remodeling we did. We may have stirred up old Crooker's ire by moving his wall, or Mrs. Crooker's, by dismantling her fruit shelves. He knew I didn't believe this; I didn't think it was the original owners. I was just saying something like it was possible. He was familiar with the lore, but he thought stuff like that just happened on the cable ghost shows, not on Pogey Point. Our problem had to be electrical, though he couldn't imagine why it had happened for a couple of weeks and then stopped, or what made it start up again a month or two later. He couldn't explain this ebb and flow cycle that began when we finished the project, and he didn't know how he felt about it if it was a ghost, so he was sticking with electrical. I asked him if he thought my electromagnetic field could somehow turn on this light; if it was me. He smiled and said "Maybe, Bright Star."

Then the activity escalated. It went beyond a simple light malfunction to a mischievous machine. I complained to David about it, told him how I would put in a load, start the cycle, and hear the water jetting into the tub, even spinning in the last few minutes, but when I went to remove the clothes they were unwashed and still dry. He thought I forgot, or I'd just *thought* I'd started the machine. He was neither interested nor supportive until one Saturday morning when he did a load of work clothes himself. A few hours later he remembered to go put them in the dryer, and called out irritated, "Hey! What'd you do, why'd you stop the wash?" I was so glad it had happened to him. I'd been waiting for the washer to fake him out because it was the only proof that would do.

"I guess you forgot to push the button," I teased him back. "Or maybe you just *thought* you did. Maybe you're pre-Alzheimer's too." He knew now what it felt like to be so unjustly accused of being derelict.

There could be no electronic reason for why the washer made the sound of doing its job when it had no such intentions, yet we'd both heard the water filling the tub, the back-and-forth churning of the wash cycle, the spin cycle, and returned to find dirty, dry clothes. "We're going to have to stand there and wait until the water starts filling the drum," I told him. "Otherwise it's just going to pretend." Neither of us could believe it was actually necessary, that it was real, and the weird precaution of having to stand over a machine to get it to do what it was supposed to had us both laughing.

The following weekend Amber came home to use the washer and it fooled her too. She was quite upset about it because she had to get to work and was planning on wearing clean clothes. I said, "See? That's what I told you about." She stood there a moment disbelieving, but she had no time for figuring it out, she had to go.

Shortly afterward, the fun with the machine stopped—the impersonation of my appliance ended just like the impersonation of David did. No more deceptive washes, no more buzzers or green lights blinking.

Maybe the new washer and dryer were just getting settled, getting the bugs out of their system, although it shouldn't have taken three years; that's how long we'd had them at the time. Or maybe the electronics were sensitive to the vibrations of the hundred-and-fifty-year-old joists. I'd even allow for some kind of draft coming up from the cellar from beneath the door; it would have had to take a U-turn for it to get to the washer, though. Maybe it was our electromagnetic fields or our auras, though I assumed I had one throughout this time that would have consistently set it off. The activity was more cyclical. But if it was a spirit using the machine to communicate, why give me such a hassle? Why cost us an hour by setting the load back? That was pretty nasty.

Since it just stopped it was easy to pass off as a bug in the system. David did, until he was made to concede there might have been something to ghosts doing things like that when he came across one at work who was also up to no good.

I mentioned earlier that David is a carpenter. For the past several years the company he works for has been remodeling the old Federal building in Bangor, and for that long, stories about the job have dominated our evening conversations. I've come to know all the key players on the project, those he likes and those he thinks are slackers, those who've stayed and those laid off, and what walls go up and what walls come down. Because construction began interfering with the courtrooms being used during the day, his work was shifted to night when the old steel and glass building comes alive with laborers, power equipment, and at least one ghost.

Dave was working alone in the basement one night and went to use one of the restrooms. The door wouldn't open; it budged an inch or two then stopped as if someone were leaning against it on the other side. He thought this strange because it was a five staller and there'd be no reason for the entryway to be blocked. As far as he knew, he was the only workman in the basement. He yelled into the room but got no answer, so once again he tried shoving the door open, this time harder. It banged against something, then came to a halt.

He wondered who was on the other side and what business they had blocking off the access. As he'd been assigned union steward, a role that wasn't admired, he reluctantly but dutifully had the responsibility of seeing that union rules were followed. He was also curious. David is no small man, his forearms have always reminded me of Popeye's after he's eaten his spinach. Determined to get to the bottom of it, he butted the door with his shoulder and finally dislodged a metal chair deliberately placed so no one could enter.

He couldn't understand how this was done without someone doing it and still being there; it had to have been done from the inside, and this was the only exit. He called out to whoever must be there, then wandered down the aisle of stalls, opening each one to find them all empty. He was trying to make sense of how the chair got where it was. It was one of those government-issue metal chairs, and it was usually on the other side of the room in a corner. Scratches on the floor showed how it had been drugged and deliberately placed to make a strong obstacle, and whoever had done it would have had to escape through the wall or the ceiling. And why? What reason would there be to it? It didn't seem like something one of the laborers would do; the guys he worked with were the "get 'er done" types; they didn't socialize enough to find a prank like this fun.

He began to wonder about pranksters of the paranormal kind.

It was then that he noticed the lighting. New recessed-can lights had just been installed and they normally lit the room brightly, but the place was dim, as if the bulbs were old and about to burn out. He'd watched enough ghost-hunting shows with me to know that spirit has the ability, if not a fondness, for communicating through electronics, like turning lights off and on. They can also drain power from lights and things like camera batteries. Something seemed to be draining the energy from the brand-new lights. Something had put the chair there. He went about his business, hoping the ghost would allow him to finish before scaring the tar out of him.

When he shared his story with the rest of the crew, hoping that one of them would speak up about having done it and be able to explain how he had, Dave was met with denial that felt genuine to him.

Every few weeks after that the ghost in the Federal building's basement continued to move the chair around the restroom. Once Dave found it facing directly into one of the stalls. But the ghost also began showing greater ability than moving a metal chair. A small dorm-size refrigerator had been stored there while the building was under construction. It was usually tucked against one of the walls so it was out of the way, but in the months that followed, the thirty-pound appliance began a habit of migrating out to the center of the room.

This experience prompted David to reconsider the idea that remodeling projects may raise the dead and that we may have had a bona fide ghost. He wasn't convinced any more than I was that this explained things like the washer's light.

Neither of us are quick to jump to supernatural causes although we allow for them in our philosophy. It wasn't until a ghost new to the other side learned to identify her through the Whirlpool, and finally succeeded in getting a message across, that I had to accept it. I knew this ghost from watching her in the flesh out the pantry window.

Thirteen

The Rosy Red Light

It began with a first impression that lasted twenty-three years.

It took place on the porch of the house only a few days after the girls and I moved in. I was standing there with my coffee mug, waving to the yellow bus as it shifted into second and groaned up Heneker Hill to the grade school, when I saw our new neighbor leave her house and walk from behind an ancient fir toward her car. She was a tiny person dressed in hospital whites. Instead of leaving as I'd expected she'd do, she surprised me by reappearing from around the tree and walking along the grassy roadside toward me.

I thought she was coming to welcome us to the neighborhood, but she only got to the telephone pole at the property line, where she stomped her orthopedic shoe down on the raised iron boundary marker. Satisfied it was firmly in place she turned back, got into the new Saab and drove away looking straight ahead as she passed me. I don't know if she intended to knock the wind out of me, but she had. She'd had to have done it for my benefit. Next-door neighbors can't help but be nosy—they've vested interests— so she had to have seen me on the porch for the past week every morning at seven thirty-five, seeing the girls off and having my coffee. I was usually waving. That day my chin was in my coffee cup.

And that's how the peculiar relationship between Betsy Ginn and me began.

The house across the street and the one next door are similar versions to mine, and at one time all three were owned by the Ginn family. The one next door to me was still occupied by a Ginn who'd inherited the fine old house. Betsy worked as a nursing supervisor at a local hospital and, like me, was a gardening fool. For the next twenty-two years we'd live side by side in similar-looking farmhouses, separated by an ancient lilac grove planted straight down the property line.

There happened to be a row of Cortland apple trees farther down this invisible fence that Jill and Amber liked climbing, just as I liked climbing apple trees as a kid; the place reminded me of our twenty-four acre farm squeezed into two. If the girls could find any fruit without worms, they'd basket it up and we'd bake a pie. We began enjoying the place the instant we got here.

But Betsy was of another mind about kids climbing apple trees and she let the girls know. She said they could damage the trees and to stay out of them, which they did after that. I suspected it had little to do with breaking limbs. Betsy was married at the time, but she'd never had kids and I don't think she liked them whether they climbed trees or not. I figured youth just rubbed Betsy the wrong way. There hadn't been any children in this part of the neighborhood for decades and she wasn't used to the energy.

But everything seemed to rub her the wrong way; there seemed so little chance of finding common ground. We had a Golden Retriever and she had cats. She'd get upset at the kids if the dog got loose and she'd harp about the leash law, though the rest of the country neighborhood seemed to share a tolerance for dogs since they owned dogs themselves. Pogey Point really should be renamed Doggy Point. Betsy never called to speak to me about things she took offense to, she only scolded the kids. When I called to address things myself she'd send over her husband Jimmy, an affable, good-natured guy who smoothed things over.

Only once did she complain to me face to face. It was when I unwittingly erred in thinking it a good thing to spruce up the lilac grove.

Now this grove, for all I know, preceded the house, because it takes a long time for a lilac bush to grow into a snarl of twelve-foot-tall twisted trees. It had great potential as a landscaping centerpiece, and I thought it deserved to be shown off. It also warranted tending as it'd been ignored for several decades and was beginning to die off inside. Though only half of the grove was on my side, the other on Betsy's, I didn't think she'd have objections if I got rid of the dead branches, or at least removed all the maples that had seeded there and were creating holes in the canopy. The overall aesthetic could be greatly improved just by raking up the decades of debris that had gathered. I came across all sorts of teenaged evidence chucked into it from the roadside; it had quite a Budweiser bottle collection through it.

One day I was working in the lilacs when Betsy arrived home from her shift and came over to give me her two cents. She didn't mind that I was willing to put in all the hard work, she just didn't trust me not to do harm, and to that end, she offered several concerns. She'd really just feel better if I left things alone. I decided that if cleaning out the neglected shrub was making her that nervous, I'd just attend to my side of it, despite the asymmetry it'd create. I'd take care of my side of the sacred boundary.

I'd never expected to be fast friends, but I had expected friendly, especially since she and I shared gardening routines. We spent our weekends in our gardens, sometimes working from morning til night, barely a hundred feet apart. I always waved to her, I'd always thought it the right thing to do with someone in that proximity, but Betsy always failed to acknowledge me. She'd find a wheelbarrow or something else handy that needed attention, and I'd return to pruning my roses or whatever I was doing, trying to recover my wind. Betsy had a way of knocking it from me.

Sadly, resenting my invisibility, I decided she had to go too. I quit waving. I ignored her right back, glad that we were just beyond speaking distance, grateful for the lilacs and weedy field separating us.

I struggled with her supposed reality that if we weren't posing a threat, we somehow didn't exist; it got my goat every time I thought about it. The only thing I could come up with for her general disapproval was my being a single parent in a lower tax bracket. I'm sure that Betsy feared I'd be unable to keep up the old house, especially without any help and on the budget of a poor grad student, and while the place probably held some sentiment having been in her family at one time, I suspected she was more concerned that my humble means and unknown character might have a negative effect on her side of the fence.

Things went on like this for the better part of our twenty-three years.

In between them, our respective households changed. Jim and Betsy divorced, and David moved in with me. Betsy was now a single parent of two cats, my two kids had flown the coop and I added a companion to my empty nest with whom she was able to improve on our history. It was a couple of winters after Jim left with his snow blower and David appeared with one, that relations between us began to change. In one winter, snow removal brought Betsy and Dave closer together than anything had in all fifteen winters she and I had shared to that point.

His going over and plowing her out gave them a reason for an association that could root a friendship. Maybe it was because they could discuss neutral things like roofing and gutters. Gutters were far more neutral than lilacs. They had practical gab fests about the weather and the egregious condos built on the old potato paddocks across the bay, and not a home improvement was missed. She declared him a hero for saving the old barn, for residing it and putting new windows in. I teased that it was because it was so much nicer to look at for her now that it didn't lean and the paint wasn't flaking. I teased that she was sucking up to the carpenter it was so handy to have move in next door.

Betsy was able to build a bridge with him, not so much to the exclusion of me, but Dave and I both felt as an easier approach to an awkward situation involving fifteen years of unneighborly behavior. It was the length of time we'd been on strike that made the use of a middleman easier for us to reapproach one another, though we never completely got over ourselves.

Then three years ago Betsy was diagnosed with brain cancer.

We kept our eye on her more often in case she needed help. She remained fairly vital until the year following her last operation, when for many months she was kept in a nursing home. On her return I baked Grandma Fluhman's old-fashioned raisin-filled cookies. They involved a lot of time so I usually only baked and distributed them to our closest neighbors at Christmas, which was how Betsy had grown fond of them. But I wasn't sure that Betsy would be around for Christmas that year. I only knew she probably needed the warmth of the gesture now, and it would give me the opportunity to let her know I was available if she ever wanted company. I thought it might be good for us if we could resolve the awkwardness between us before she left the planet.

Her caregiver, a local woman, answered the door. It was the first time in twenty-three years I'd been in Betsy Ginn's house. She was a waif sitting in the kitchen against a window over a colonial drop-leaf table. She smiled to see me, apologizing for being a mess. She was surprisingly self-conscious, telling me she didn't like not looking her best and she didn't like folks she knew seeing her that way. I said we were all messes. The local woman chuckled and Betsy smiled and relaxed. I offered to read to her sometime if she'd like it, or if she ever felt in the mood to talk. I was interested in what she knew of the history of Pogey Point and the Ginn houses. It seemed to me to be a subject that could neutralize our own history.

I was aware of how tired she was, and asked if I could give her a hug before I left. She smiled with tears, and we embraced for the first, last, and only time in our decades as neighbors. I told her we loved her and I realized I meant it. I realized, too, how extra-long the hug seemed for a woman with guarded boundaries.

On my way out, I looked for the red light I always saw in her window from across the field. My pantry window overlooks a wildflower garden under the apple tree next to the barn, the view then opens out into the field and her house, just skirting the lilac grove. After dark, there was always a soft rosy light crossing the field that came from her kitchen window. I'd always assumed there must be a hanging Tiffany lamp above the sink where I sometimes saw her doing dishes, but the light I'd imagined wasn't there; what I'd seen was a small table lamp with a colored glass shade sitting on her cabinet. This was the rosy light I'd been seeing those past twenty-three years. It was actually like meeting an old friend.

Betsy died a week and a half later, two weeks before Christmas. I was glad I didn't wait on the cookies or the hug. The night of her funeral I was standing in the pantry, looking across the field to the stately old house all lit up like it was expecting company. Over the years I'd admired Betsy's exterior lighting. In summer the floodlights illuminated the tall white house against expanses of green, and in winter the house merged into bright drifts of deep snow. I would have liked her to know the joy it brought me to have such a Currier and Ives shot from my window. I wished I'd gone over and told her, and how much I enjoyed the lone little spruce in the middle of the field she lit up each Christmas.

I had the feelings a neighbor contemplating the end of the relationship had—present to the notion that though Betsy and I had kept our distance, we were a lot on each other's minds. Her kitchen window looked my way and my pantry window looked back, enabling us to traverse the sacred lilac boundary without liability. We'd abutted each other's little patch of earth for most of our lives and had exchanged energy every one of those days, without ever getting involved. I mourned the loss in the hundreds of days over the twenty-three years that we'd silently gardened within a hundred feet of one another.

The following night I was at the window again, only now I was looking out into blank, dark space. Betsy's house had disappeared, not even the little kitchen light was left on. I was startled by the absolute evaporation of both house and individual. It was shocking not to have a light on over there after all these years, an adjustment for me but cruel to Betsy, and, just as I was thinking how much she wouldn't have liked it, I heard a buzz. The washer light came on by itself for the first time in a year. This time there was no guessing about mechanical failures because I immediately sensed a presence, the way I had when I was looking for lily vases that day and the washer suddenly blinked on right next to me, as if to reach out and touch me. Only on the day I was scouting for a jar for the lilies, I had no idea who it was.

I'd always suspected there was more than one spirit who'd learned to use the Whirlpool's light, because each cycle of activity had its own personality. Sometimes the light would come back on right after I'd gone and turned it off, sometimes it was more considerate, only coming on once or twice a day. Then came the faked sounds, the spin cycle for instance. Sometimes all I heard was the buzzer, the light didn't necessarily respond with it. And the timing between intervals varied, I was never able to correlate the occurances with a moon or weather cycle, or household energy levels—the peaks and lows in a marriage. It seemed an arbitrary thing, a willed phenomena.

Though it had begun years before Betsy died, I felt she was the one communicating now. "Are you here, Betsy?" I asked the dim pantry, my eyes watching the light to see what happened. I'd seen it go on before but never shut itself off, so if it did, I'd have to consider it a direct response to the question. Spirits could communicate through flashlights and K2 meters this way. While I'd seen this sort of thing happen on the cable shows, nothing prepared me for when it actually happened. When the light blinked out I thought, *Oh my, what now?*

Since I'd started the conversation, I asked what she wanted, my eyes glued to the light, somewhere betwixt expecting it to respond and not really wanting it to. When it didn't, I realized it wouldn't have done much good if it had because I hadn't asked a yes or no question. I tried reformulating one. Was she there to square with me; was it to resolve things between us before she moved on? When the light failed to make this affirmative, I felt a little silly assuming I'd be on her mind, and silly that I was talking to the pantry in the middle of the night. I was actually hoping Betsy wasn't around to see my foolishness.

I looked back out the window, jarred again by the missing house. Why *did* it jar me so? Why did I hurt for Betsy, understand it as a personal affront? Why did I care? Was it Betsy's upset that I was feeling? Jackpot. The light buzzed on in direct answer and I stood there staring with disbelief at what was usually a pretty trivial thing.

I told Dave about it when he got home at four in the morning. "No way," he said. He asked if I could have bumped the washer. I told him facetiously that I was not big enough to have made contact with it from across the room, and concluded what a freaky thing it was for the washing machine to have answered me. At that point I was convinced the washer acted as Betsy's new middleman. Dave found it strange that I'd make the claim; even for me it was pretty far out there. But I was firm about what I thought Betsy wanted. "Think about it," I said. "It is totally in character for Betsy to be offended by her house vanishing like that." I reminded him how attached she was to the place and how she worried about appearances. The place was her presentation to the world, her imprint on the planet. One little light, that was all she wanted; it was the old tradition of keeping a candle burning.

He told me *my* attachment to the lights was the issue. If Betsy could turn on the light on the washer why was she having so much trouble with the one on her porch? I'd thought of that, too, but I still knew this was more than separation anxiety.

For the next few nights this sort of thing continued whenever I was looking across the field to the unlit house. By then the house was lurking in the shadowy light of a cloud-striped full moon, which improved matters a little, but I wasn't feeling any relief from Betsy. Whenever I thought of her or the house, the washer light would respond, either immediately or within a few minutes. It was the most activity we'd had for a while, certainly the most direct, and its timing was hard to dismiss as unrelated to Betsy's recent death. By the end of the week I was wondering who I could contact to turn on her lights.

Dave still maintained that it was me alone feeling the distress of the dark house, something I had to honestly evaluate. I hadn't seen the house dark in twenty-three years, so I confessed to having to adjust, but an adjustment was different from an obsession, and it hadn't become one until the washer had gotten involved. I could live without the light next door but apparently Betsy couldn't. I didn't know why she picked on me, why she didn't inspire someone closer to her, but she expected me to act. David suggested I stay out of the pantry.

I did try and stay away from the pantry whenever possible, but no matter where I was, I got drawn to look out other windows that viewed the house next door. Something unusual was drawing my attention to it and the matter seemed to grow more urgent with time. One night I was standing behind the zebra plant and looking through the leafless lilac grove. This window was in the parlor, and unlike the one in the pantry that skirted the grove in favor of the field, this one looked straight at the sacred boundary. I was wondering what I could do to settle this distraction. I thought of calling Jimmy, who'd maintained a close relationship with Betsy and the property. It occurred to me that I actually had his number; he'd given it to me when Betsy came back from the nursing home, in case of an emergency or something. I couldn't remember where I'd put it. I never thought I'd use it, so it might take some time to find. It satisfied me as a good enough excuse to forget about the house next door for the night.

The following evening I was passing the "phone booth"—which is what I call the colonial jelly cabinet in the kitchen that houses the phone, phone books, and business supplies—and my eye caught a blue slip of paper wedged under an address book. It was Jim's number, and I wasn't all that pleased to see it. I now felt a duty to call him and suggest he come out to the house and turn on some lights. I supposed I could have reasoned it in the interest of neighborhood safety—a dark house was a target for hoodlums. This way I could leave out Betsy completely, but I didn't really want to be the one to suggest it in case he couldn't be bothered.

It was too late in the evening to call so I promised myself to call the next day. In the meantime, I'd try experimenting with telepathy to see if I could spare myself the trouble. I'd been somewhat successful at this. I settled comfortably into the captain's chair and closed my eyes, concentrating on sending an image. *Jim, go down to Betsy's and turn on a light*. I visualized him: handsome, with salt-and-pepper hair. I imagined Betsy. *Jimmy, come to Stockton and turn on the light, it's dangerous for the house to be dark.* I visualized the house, trying to draw his thoughts to Pogey Point. I tried instilling a sense of worry for the place, I wanted him annoyed so he'd pay attention. *Jim, Betsy's light.* I visualized the rosy lamp.

The next morning when I got to the bottom of the stairs I saw Jim's car parked in Betsy's drive. *Wow, did I really get through?* I was amused. Maybe he'd just come down to check the place, it'd been a week and we'd had snow. Right, I could see him shoveling. I decided to go speak to him after I'd gotten coffee, but by the time it was ready he was gone and I was kicking myself for not having taken my chance. Why didn't I discharge my duty and go over, robe and all? Now I *would* have to call. This time I'd have to go the normal route.

I took my mug into the pantry to catch the morning sunlight easing above the roof of the barn and lighting up the rooster on the weathervane. I usually tried to catch this magical time each morning, attended by my remarkable coffee mug, the one that had lasted me all these years, all through the kids—the same one I was using that morning long ago when a white nurse's shoe met with an iron peg. How could I end up missing Betsy so much, someone who had the knack of knocking the wind out of me?

I smiled at myself and went to warm the coffee, returning to the window. Just when I passed the washer tucked in its little cove, the light blinked on. It made me smile thinking how relentless Betsy was, and wonder whether she'd heard my question. I also appreciated how disappointed she must have been in me. Well, I'd do what I could for her later. Now I wanted to suck in the chilly winter sunlight and re-energize myself. I needed resonance.

And I got it, the kind that takes your breath away.

I had to shade my eyes from the sun's interference to verify it, but the familiar red glow across the wintering field was there. Somehow, *this thing had happened. There you go, old friend,* I told her, *The light will be there tonight and for as long as the house is empty.* I waited to see if the washer's light went off as a way of verifying our communication, but it didn't, and after a minute or two of thanking the Universe for spiritual opportunities like this, and my ability to appreciate them, I went over and shut the washer light off. My Whirlpool hasn't spoken to me since.

Fourteen

Taking Back My Ghosts

The odds tell us we're not alone in the universe and I firmly believe it. No astrophysicist today would say Earth is the apple of the universe's eye or that we are its sole inhabitants, though they're pretty sure that the sole intelligences on Earth are in human or physical form. I think the difference in accepting there are other unknown sentient beings at large with capability of communication, and the idea of ghosts with that capability, is based on a limited view of a three-dimensional technological world. It's easier to believe there are other beings on other planets because we're comfortable thinking in terms we're familiar with or at least can imagine—things we're more likely to understand and relate to as physical beings—aliens are more scientific, more apt to be, because they are living.

It's harder to accept dead people. Even though dead is a local idea that relates only to bodies that are temporary applications of energy, the permanence of spirit man is much less likely to many folks than corporeal beings of fantastic imagination that *can* die.

I haven't had experience with aliens from other planets, but I have with beings from a spiritual dimension that may or may not surround our own, may or may not be here all the time—but at least some of the time they are and they're very much "alive." Those without their own experiences have a right to be skeptical, but those of fair minds may admit that part of the problem is that for so long in man's history the domain of the dead has been the domain of religion. So was and still is in many cases the practice of medicine or the study of astronomy. It's an emotional blockage more than a rational one, and might be overcome by mitigating religion's righteous fervor to karmic indifference, and beings who aren't indifferent to the human race.

The paranormal is a broad category involving phenomena that can't be explained within the limits of three dimensions—four, if we include time. Quantum physics assures us there is a relationship between the visible and invisible and is looking for the mechanism that exchanges information between these dimensions. Problems with electrons popping in and out of existence, or entanglement, where electrons appear to respond to one another though separated by tremendous distances, imply a level of consciousness is involved in this transference of energy through space. If energy or consciousness cannot be destroyed, then the dead have their own technology and it's intellectually irresponsible to deny beings a place at the table simply because we don't relate to them.

This chapter concludes with a simple idea and science likes simple ideas. Parsimony is the rule by which science selects its beliefs; this is based on the way the Universe appears to work simply and without too many contingencies: A modern view of the relationship between the Universe and Earth harkening back to the medieval alchemists' credo, "As above, so below." So, where there is indecisive data for phenomena, cases where the jury's still out but there are a host of possible explanations, usually the theory with the least number of variables and "if and/or buts" wins out as accepted truth.

I wonder if there is any simpler assumption than "We survive death." It appears to be a natural assumption, an instinct in humans that predates both civilization and modern man. It follows that if consciousness survives then communication is possible between states of being. We see this in primitive traditions; primitive, not in the pejorative sense, but primal. That "the ancestors" are there seems to be a built-in assumption, rather than a sophisticated lie primal man told to himself for comfort. Being hunters and on close terms with nature, there seems no reason to me to think that they would have thought of the death of humans any differently than any other creature. To make up a survival mythology would be sophistication. I think there is reason to say that the instinct was there first, although reason is intent on fighting it.

The means of contact, the technology used between states or dimensions is incredibly simple, perhaps too simple to be taken seriously. One may need space technology to connect to sentient beings on other planets, but one only has to think to be in another state. My experience lends the idea strength by showing how fluid the exchange between the fields keeping us in our places can be, and puts ghosts rightfully among the denizens of the universe.

This final story is actually a succession of stories building upon this relationship between the living and spirit. Up to this point many of my experiences seemed to just happen to me; here I initiate the relationship, showing how it is literally possible to have a relationship with beings we call angels, guides, ghosts, or spirits, who exist in a place we've been for ages calling heaven. As I said in the beginning, you have to understand the spiritual details, not just take in the verbs of an experience like this, simply because of the nature of the transaction. For me the experience tends to be highly sensitive to situation and occurs through a sort of unwitting dialogue—without appreciating how thought is the technology of the conscious "dead," the experience can be mistaken as monologue private to oneself.

It begins on a haunted blueberry barren.

Heneker Hill sits above our village and grants one of the finest views of Penobscot Bay. From there, the view extends beyond the cape to Castine, and farther out and along the island-littered coast. The hill is mostly forest, but there's a bald spot on the top that the forest surrounds. In this clearing is a gigantic barren strewn with glacial debris, and granite boulders the size of houses litter the field like a giant child's marbles. It's quiet up there, a great place to meditate your situation in this world and your relationship to the other. Barrens in Maine have an austere beauty that remind me of parts of Connemara, and whether or not an imagined ancestral setting is important in the scheme of things, Heneker Hill is where the next story starts.

It was a perfect September Saturday when David and I took our baskets up to the hill. We were hoping to scrounge for what was left of the berries after raking was over, as many locals do. It had been my choice to come, the way I wished to spend my fifty-sixth birthday. I wanted to spend this fine morning soaking in the late summer sun and taking my place in nature, competing with the bears, birds, and deer for the last of the berries, which I paid back with the apples and pears from my little orchard. When we'd treated ourselves enough to this adventure, we'd go down the lane and have bacon and blueberry pancakes with Maine maple syrup for my birthday supper.

We parked the Dodge Ram down the hill at the gate and hiked to the top, enjoying the weather and view before getting to business. The blueberries were sparse but on the edges of the field and in its gullies there was wealth untouched by the raking equipment. Soon we'd wandered away from one another; he took to the higher ground, I went toward the lower. It was a day that inspired song in the heart and mine was singing. I was thanking God for this beautiful birthday, and for the chance to share it with someone I enjoyed and cared about. I was thankful to be a daughter of the Universe, grateful to be a unit of consciousness whose experience has been of Earth. The best birthday gift a girl can have is feeling right with herself, and I was thinking my fifty-sixth birthday was the best I'd ever had.

As I moved lower down the hill, further into my own thoughts, I sensed that two women had joined me. I immediately thought of Grandma and Mom because of what the day meant. It wasn't going to be the ordinary birthday if I followed through on the restless decision I'd secretly come to the mountain to settle. The choice taken today would actually signify a rebirth. At such earthly moments the attendance of my mother and grandmother seemed proper and their support welcome. In their world there was time for everything, and if nothing was missed then heaven's indifference to birthdays was human artifact.

Besides, picking blueberries was something we'd enjoyed doing together; I felt their kindred spirit in the thought and could easily imagine them there with their baskets. I had the surprising impression they were *giggling*, something out of character. The energy wasn't that of solemn women, but was of the joyful kind associated with youth. It was also extremely contagious. I felt myself expanding out into the world and realized that *this was what joy did*.

I looked up to make sure none of this glorious experience was showing, that I wasn't glowing or something, and found Dave completely unaware and busy at work, kneeling in the scrub around a gigantic boulder high up near the tree line. Then I went back to looking for the affirmation I was hoping to find among the blueberries in the sunlit gullies—half a century of batting the idea about hadn't made it any friendlier to assurances, maybe I had to be on my knees to find that affirmation. This good feeling I had was only a good start to the conviction I needed. I knew that on nice days like this when everything was swell, good feelings could be temporary. It was a good start on my way, but I needed the confidence to last longer than a day to see me through the rough patch ahead—something nearly guaranteed when giving up a day job.

For most of my professional life I'd been teaching. For the last nine years I had been at the private school knowing that while for the most part I enjoyed the work, I'd only found the most compatible way of supporting myself until I could do what I really wanted. The work suited me. I was good at establishing rapport with teenagers and kids labeled "difficult," and I felt good, as all teachers should, about what I was doing to create a better society. But it didn't scratch the itch. I wanted to write and feared going to my grave still itching.

"Hey, hon!" I heard David call. I stood up from behind the boulder I was working around. "There you are, I couldn't see ya. Oughta come up here by me." I told him I'd work my way back up from down here, that I had stuff to do. He walked higher up, and I decided I'd exploited the berries well enough in the area I was at and wandered farther downhill to see what I could find elsewhere. I was thinking how the desire to write was really more a part of chemistry than an itch, how I'd wanted to put word to paper before I could read or write. I was making up stories for Rodney, my no-more-the-wiser smaller brother, out of Dad's old church history books as soon as I could lift them.

Mom said I came installed with a writer's imagination; an inheritance I attributed to Grandma who shared both the dream and vocation, unlike Mother who said the writing bug had skipped her generation. This was a lie of humility as it turned out. After her death when her numerous journals were available to us and I'd had a chance to read through them, I learned a lot about this woman I called Mom, who might have been a writer had circumstances been more kind. Mom hadn't avoided infection, she just drove it underground in order to survive, as her twenty-some-odd books of life made clear.

I paused in my berry scouting to assess the situation. My spiritual companions seemed to be leading my thoughts to this place. Never before had I included Mother or Grandmother in on my decision or thought what it might have meant to them; it'd always been a private tussle. It occurred to me that this was somewhat of a joint venture, that these unseen women whose joy turned serene as the morning crossed into afternoon had passed on a longing that had yet to stir from seed in the family line, and their presence reflected their vested earthly interest in how it would all work out for me. Spirit beings have interest in the planet and its players because it is the place they've chosen to incarnate, sometimes in familial lines but always within a history. What I did now might affect the skin they would come to live in.

They'd empathized with this longing I'd so badly fought lately, had all but snuffed out with marriages, kids, divorces, and house payments, despite early publishing success at eighteen. Mother would say I'd missed the boat when she'd offered me that crack at journalism. I'd held this longing at bay, until I was reinspired by a dear friend I was fortunate to find in the old matriarch of the Romany family I stayed with during my fieldwork days.

Dora was so loveable and uniquely traditional among modern Gypsies that I wanted to write about her as much as she wanted me to tell her story. Even so, life was just as much in the way then as it had been before and what attention I could pay to any writing project was brief.

It would go on this way unless I chose a different possibility for myself.

I stood up from where I'd been kneeling in the shrubbery to give my legs a stretch. The sun on the bay seemed reflected toward me and I tried sucking it all in. This September day on a hilltop that looked like Connemara, I must allow myself the completion to satisfy this generational longing, whether school stays or not.

I heard Dave calling. I thought he thought we were about done. He was climbing up the side of a boulder to enjoy the sun and the view before heading back to the truck. I stretched my back; I'd almost had enough myself. I turned uphill toward him, veering to my right, thinking I'd casually pick berries on my way back to the tote road, when something caught my eye in the woods' shadows at the barren boundary. It impressed me as a light, several of them, moving, that was my first notion of it—orbs—but my mind accounted for it more likely being sunglass glare. Whatever it was retreated before I could get a good look at it, as if whatever it was wished to draw my eye and make me aware of my surroundings, but not put on a show. It could have been a deer or a small animal, I told myself; I hoped it wasn't a bear or a moose.

I scanned the tree line that surrounded us and forced myself to be honest. *It had been a light, a few of them.* In the shadows I'd not have been able to detect an animal's eyes unless they were reflective, and it was too highly elevated to be a pair or two of eyes. I'd sensed Dave and I weren't alone as soon as we'd gotten there. Even after establishing Grandmother and Mother's presence, I was aware that there were others who were holding to the background.

I worked my way slowly back to the tote road feeling that spirits circled the barren in the tree line, and decided it was enough affirmation for me, where I was at, to take as a green light from heaven. Before moving onto the road that David was coming down, with Grandma and Mother as witnesses, I took a leap of faith in my relationship to words and the notion that chronicling life was what I had put myself here to do. There was no turning back then; I'd crossed the Rubicon of promises made to oneself and dear friends.

Dave was boasting his lot, waving his basket at me as he closed in. If he'd done as well as I had then we'd have surplus enough after pancakes to make us a pie.

After I put in my resignation later that month, and during the months I waited for a replacement to be hired, this confident and highly hopeful frame of mind continued. To help maintain it I fantasized about my new life. It would be peaceful. I'd take early morning walks with Zoe down to the old pier and check out the tidal pools. I'd get to know people I hadn't time to meet before. I'd slow down and enjoy life and sunrises, read and write unhindered by the fire. Now that I had the time to think in one straight uninterrupted line, the novel I'd been working on in spates for fifteen years was going to finally come together.

I began enthusiastically in January, but soon ran into trouble. The problem was that, over time, between what brief stretches of dabbling with it I could afford, my ideas for the book had evolved, a euphemism for "wandered all over the place." What began as an idea for a fieldwork memoir of an old-school Gypsy matriarch became a novel with Gypsies in it, secondary to ghosts I'd robbed from my jars and a main character who'd come to very much resemble me. I cut myself some slack, and honestly went into it believing that straightening it all out was doable.

The manuscript ended up giving me a surprising amount of trouble. It boiled down to an ethical crisis I ran into when trying to tease the character Vera and myself apart, while trying to keep the ghosts. As I got more seriously into the experiences I'd chosen for her, I began to feel they weren't that transferrable. The ghosts didn't seem to "work" without me because the meaning was in the situation, even if they were patterned on the real thing. The ghosts in Vera's world were having a difficult time living up to their potential.

I didn't know why it hadn't bothered me before, but it occurred to me from the editing I was doing that I'd cheapened the souls who'd inspired these creatures of fiction by disowning them. Not only did I feel like I was ruffling their feathers, I was doing a disservice to my great little town and a great bunch of characters. By scrubbing out the personal details and spiritual contexts that Vera couldn't use, these hybrid ghosts had turned disappointingly frail and didn't amount to anything really worth writing home about. What had been empowering experiences for me had become spirits powerless to testify of their reality, bound to a make-believe world. The proof was in my pudding, not Vera's.

Still. I couldn't let the truth bother me. I wasn't writing a memoir, I was writing a novel, which I'd put too much time into not to see through. I was totally committed to it after fifteen years; I was the little engine that could, eventually. Now that I had this chance, the one I'd been aching for, I just had to have confidence that I'd find some way around this crisis of legitimacy with more time and creative determination. And to do this, I couldn't allow the real actors to get to me. This dissatisfaction that decided to emerge right in the middle of things—linked to this idea that I was short-changing spirit by bowing out—had to be tabled for now. Even so, there were evenings working late in the captain's chair beside a richly coaled hearth when I stopped typing and looked up to observe an unquestionably haunted parlor. On those nights when David was working the night shift and Zoe and I were home alone, I could sometimes imagine ourselves surrounded by the ghosts I'd shelved.

With David's oppositional attitude toward the whole writing affair, that like his namesake and predecessor, I began privately doubting myself when things continued to be muddled. By summer I was rethinking my whole religion —whether I'd been mistaken about this inheritance, or maybe I liked the idea of writing better than the reality; it was actually miserable work. The peacefulness I'd imagined a year ago was marred with top-shelf anxiety and, on the cusp of depression, I stopped walking the dog to the pier and getting up for sunrises, contracting instead of expanding into the world as the year went on. With October came crushing doubts, in November my confidence completely tanked, and by December I was brought to my knees seeking straight answers.

It was a windy, dark night in Crooker's little farmhouse; the fire was going, a candle was burning. I was working on the novel, but I only had one foot in it, the other was there in the parlor. I blamed the wind for stirring up distraction; I wasn't accomplishing anything because there seemed to be too much happening. I put the laptop down on the hassock and went to stoke the fire, thinking about Laura, a friend of Ruth's I'd met at a Halloween wine tasting she'd hosted at the Keeper's Cottage the year before. Laura had the "gift."

I didn't know this when we introduced ourselves to each other in the kitchen, but I was stunned when Laura immediately congratulated me on my decision to quit teaching to write. It was surprising that a complete stranger would know about it. I didn't cut that broad a swathe in local society; I had to assume that Ruth had told her about me, though Ruth wasn't the kind to go around talking about other people's business. Before I could ask Laura how she knew of my plans, she told me she admired my guts, it took courage to take the bull by the horns at *our* age. This time I was stunned by two things. First, "the bull by the horns," it was something Mom used to say and I hadn't heard it in ages.

But the biggest stunner was her remark about our ages, it seemed like deliberate charity because I could easily ball park her about ten years younger, and I'd felt this sort of deliberateness before in approval at the supermarket. I was a little taken aback by the whole brief encounter, especially in light of its association and timing. Here I was at another junction, turning another corner. Beings like this did exist in the flesh!

Ruth denied she'd said anything about it, that it was just Laura—she picked up on things, which was why she made such a good healer. Her keen psychic abilities had helped clear the Keeper's Cottage of its ghosts way back when.

I lugged another stick of maple out of the wood box and cast it on top of the coals. Laura told me the way it would go, she could sense my worry and thought to comfort me but didn't spare me the truth. She said there'd be some kind of interference with the writing at first, trouble for about a year, then things would smooth out. I hadn't liked hearing it, but now that the year was nearly past I hoped it was true.

Returning to the captain's chair I was feeling all bottled up, like I just needed to sit there and cry. The book shouldn't have been giving me this sort of trouble. It was a story about a woman living on an island surrounded by a bunch of Victorian dead people, after all this time why hadn't I figured out what needed to happen? Hell, at the beginning I had a straight shot to the end line, the whole ending scene, now I wasn't sure of tomorrow. *Had I dreamt too big for my britches?*

I knew I was projecting my inner turmoil onto the page and that was why I was in limbo: I guessed I hadn't gotten the green light from heaven on the barren after all; I'd always had a permissive imagination. I guess I had on rose-colored glasses that day so as not to notice I'd already reached my earning-career peak; something like that might have called for a self-induced attack of blueberry euphoria. Was I so thoroughly wrong about myself and my history of desire? Thinking how it ran through my life like a main artery yet not being my chemistry—simply a frustrated romantic's excuse to long for something—was a crushing thing to have to come to grips with.

Restless, I got up and went to stir the fire that didn't need it. Poking at embers and resituating logs sometimes helped me think. There was a quarrel going on and I was both of the combatants. I was mad at myself for what appeared to be a lifelong deception, and about the discovery that I couldn't rely on myself; somewhere else I was thinking, *Yeah but hold on …*

I left the hearth and headed for the kitchen, thinking that a glass of boxed wine was called for. I got the wine but didn't drink it; I felt sour enough. I was standing in front of the double-wide old-fashioned aluminum farmhouse sink where Hyrum Crooker had placed a horizontal window. It viewed the gardens and orchard and a good deal of the night sky. It's sort of magical to have the universe spread out in front of the kitchen sink like that; Old Hyrum was a magical sort of guy considering the brook in the basement. Any magic I might have had seemed to have run its course. Prayer in the past year had grown into constant discourse. I felt impotent and betrayed that things hadn't gone better; faith just seemed to set one up for disappointment. Just how far could prayer get a person? I guessed there must be a limit.

I was speaking to the Milky Way when I expressed my confusion out loud. I asked the moon what the big joke on Jinnit Girl was about, feeling sorry for myself and getting no pleasure from it. I needed to get a handle on things in a desperate sort of way. Not waiting one more self-deluded minute, I braced against the sink for some clarity in the matter, ready to take on anything that bubbled up from the subconscious. My time with Jack sprang back. It was one particular part I keyed in on, the point where I was pouting to Cornstarch girl my disappointment in a similar ideal and then that guy turned the aisle corner just as I was turning one in attitude. It had been a moment of consequence to my future, and ever since then I'd counted on there being wiser and more benevolent beings than humans to help sort out the rough patches. Well, if there really were interested parties that could help me think straight, *where the hell were they? At the grocery store? Where was the gang from up on the mountain now?*

Maybe there are piddly people and I'm one of them.

I turned and faced into the kitchen and through it, out the cross-paned window on the other side that viewed the front porch. The honeysuckle vine had obscured the railing in the twenty-three years since I'd planted it, now in December its twisting hardwood provided a delicate lattice for snow. I was admiring its loveliness when I felt something shift in the geometry of the room. I had the impression that a force had moved through the glass and was bringing the outside in, as if that portion of the porch wall had suddenly gone supple. I worried that the December chill would flood in, but felt no sudden temperature difference, just the sensation I got in the presence of spirit.

Over half a century I've gotten to know how this feels and I can appreciate what is happening. It's really a pleasant thing most of the time; it all seems fairly normal, though I'm very aware of what an exceptional experience it is and that's delightful. For me it's a sudden understanding that another intelligence is with me. You know when you're alone—you're familiar with your own energy. Instincts easily sense self from other; you can tell when you're responding to another personality because you feel a relationship.

Knowing I'd finally caught *someone's* attention, it seemed the perfect time to plead my case, but apparently they'd heard it all before, because quicker than I could think-speak it, a voice said, "It's two books." I couldn't see this spirit in detail but strongly sensed it was male, and I knew where to direct my attention. I knew he was standing right inside the window facing me because he emerged from there and the snow came through brighter on one side of the pane than on the other. It would have been unnoticeable if I hadn't just been looking there and suddenly saw the smudge in the light; it meant ghosts had subtle mass. I sensed he was an important person to me, someone who knew me quite well, perhaps my guide, *that angel.*

I sensed others had joined us less dramatically. I could distinguish different energy fields and knew they were expressions of personalities. Two female spirits were leaning against the breakfront counters side by side, they seemed an affable pair and I had the thought that they *traveled* together. Another presence stood in the doorway next to Zoe's water bowl. I sensed it was a male mostly because he thought he should be there but didn't really want to get involved. I had the idea that he was put off with me for not figuring things out for myself, so maybe it was Dad. I could only guess at their identities, but for the most part they seemed upbeat and encouraging, even teasing me a little, reminding me, perhaps because I'd just been thinking of them, of the folks I'd run into at the grocery.

I seemed to have an immense capacity for suffering, some was good but this was needless. This was the first thing communicated, then some inference that I was stalling. *I should lighten up, the sky wasn't falling, and I knew better.* I don't know if all this was transmitted in these precise words, but something like gentle criticism was.

At any rate, my self-concern outweighed their opinion or my curiosity about them; I was more interested in this notion of two books. I assumed it referred to the novel's ambitious plot, which I'd been struggling to pare down. I'd removed some sixty pages of self-intrusion so far, and knew when those sixty pages came to mind that, considering what they described, they contained material for this other book, a book about *real* things—like *this,* real people like me having a fit in my kitchen in a desperate effort to squeeze editorial advice out of trustworthy folks from the other side.

Then I suddenly switched tracks and became aware that the wind had died down and the kitchen had become roomier. I was alone with the breakfront cupboards.

This haunting began and ended with affirming presences who saw fit to mute the boundaries of the playing field at a time when I needed something to keep me going. It may sound Pollyanna-ish to suggest that all spirit beings are good-natured and helpful, but fortunately this has largely been my experience. I can't speak to the darker kind of spirit because I've only known one bad apple and even then I felt

I'd profited. It may seem desperately misguided to think that folks going about their business on the other side would drop things to respond to a temper tantrum. But they did.

I don't know if those folks on the barren followed me home that day. It doesn't matter their details, what matters is my testimony of a spirit-assist in my unexpected year of coming to terms with Vera. If not for her, I would not have reckoned the value in my jars, and if not for them, you wouldn't be nearing the end of the *other* book that describes ways the universe joins physical and spiritual energy fields through consciousness, and how with emotion and intent focused in thought, you can get ghosts to walk out of walls to help through the rough patches we design for ourselves.

This isn't that miraculous, and sometimes isn't all that enlightening.

It wasn't the first time I'd been inspired to look at the editing situation another way. When my experiences lost their luster for Vera I realized they weren't suited to fiction. I did know better. What "two books" signified was a personal way of communicating to me that I had a green light to act on the idea that had bothered me since I began withdrawing from the text; succumbing to the parlor haunt would satisfy everyone better, but I wasn't game yet. I saw the possibility in my edits, knew that as I exited Vera's world the ghosts were coming with me. I'd had ghost-surround for a year in my parlor egging me on, but what I wanted was their show of support. I wasn't afraid of big britches—I was afraid of not filling them out as well as I could and for that I wanted the other half's cooperation.

I probably had been stalling, but I had good reasons behind the original hesitations that led me to use Vera as proxy in the first place. One was an ethical concern around the intensely private matter of spirituality. I didn't want to feel as if I was exploiting it, uneasy about it being mistaken for an entertainment and exposing my convictions to the cynicism that going public would risk. It was better for Vera to take the brunt. Another concern had to do with reliability. There were two *real* sides to this story; I had to own the obligation to get the ghost right, an obligation I didn't have when these experiences were presented as fiction.

I took this as seriously as any biographer would. I didn't want the ruffling of too many ghost feathers. If ghosts are the next stage beyond this life, eventually I'd have to account for myself. Those who'd guided and comforted me in times of transition, in situation or awareness, or nudged me back on plan by reminding me—when I'd forgotten with my already full-enough life—that this other dimension was there, were obviously people who'd continued a relationship with me despite our present material differences. They deserved better treatment. They deserved their reality back as beings of humor and helpfulness, and wanted, I believe, the fluidity of the veil known so that men might be empowered by their attendance.

Now *that* was something to write home about.

It was a serious matter to take on. Intimidating because to grasp the truth of what had happened I'd have to take on the fruit room, and it was a damned scary place. All bottled up, I wasn't sure what kinds of things I'd find to write about once I truly got looking. I'd never fully squared with the past, I'd only selected from it a few useful jars that I had no ambition to explore except as source material. Over the years I might have grown rusty at sensing light bulb strings in the dark. Social reaction was of some relevance; Jill and Amber had been gracious enough about their mother writing Victorian ghost stories, but what would they say about true paranormal? There were all sorts of halfway reasonable excuses not to want to tell my story up front rather than between the lines, but clearly I'd been working up to doing it.

I pondered this new commitment. It'd take guts to start something new, something like this. David would interpret it as failure, if not an embarrassing, self-exposing thing to do. My heart sank when I thought of actually beginning a new project with such low spirits and vitality. I knew this could be transient optimism, still I'd asked for help and they'd told me to lighten up and the sky wouldn't fall. Besides, if Laura was right, then hell was nearly over.

It was a still and very cold night at Crooker's in early January. The January before, I'd been eager to get going on a manuscript that had acquired seventy thousand words; now facing a blank page I was hesitating. It was already past midnight.

Having spirit beings in your kitchen, more or less encouraging you to tell their stories while at the same time handing you superb material, doesn't seem like the sort of experience that would wear off. But the idea of starting a new book wasn't spared the usual zigzags in optimism.The kitchen visitation had taken place before the holidays and over the holidays I'd come to have second thoughts of whether this book would make any better sense than the other. If I was any more capable of writing nonfiction than fiction. A good deal of the original certainty sobered when my family reacted to the idea with the skepticism I'd feared.

But the real burr was that after my fifteen-year relationship with Dave, I felt insecure with my decision to relegate Vera to the back burner. I hadn't just been committed to the project, I'd been devoted. Even though the mention of two books comforted me around the novel's worth and increased the likelihood I'd return to it, putting it aside looked and felt like giving up. It was precisely because I was afraid of facing another dreadful year that I was hung up on the promise I'd made to myself—and intended to take seriously—that if I began even so much as a page of this new project I'd see it through to publication. I'd been sure of the novel, too, when I'd started. I had to be more careful this time.

This final story starts at the hearth and like many of the others have, it involves a window.

I was sweeping up the polished granite hearth with my hand-tied bramble broom, amusing myself by telling any ghost that was interested in being famous that they'd have to help me strike up the confidence to begin the first page. I was past the sky falling and all that tormented writer jazz; I just wanted my confidence reassured. I needed to know that I hadn't been mistaken about my interpretation of the jars now that I was getting down to the nitty-gritty of putting them to page. If I was going to write something honest, it had to be an honest process, and I figured that one more good dose of heavenly affirmation wouldn't be asking too much before I dug in and got to work.

I returned the broom to its corner and laid some drier logs on the coals to nurse the fire back to life. If I was really going to do this thing I'd be up the rest of the night once I got started. Rekindling the fire was an optimistic gesture, if not something of a ritual one. I watched until the delicate white-paper birch bark caught fire and the coals were humming again, not summoning anyone to make another appearance or to even give me a sign; a peaceful satisfied feeling would be good enough. It was my job to argue my options, theirs to give me their blessing. I knelt to enjoy the companionship of the fire and see what gave. The cursor sat blinking.

Now warmed and a bit more disarmed, I moved to the parlor window that's in the corner of the L the farmhouse makes. It has become the zebra's window, for the five-foot plant feeds greedily from the southern sunlight it provides during winter. This window shares the kitchen's honeysuckle porch but stretches its view out to the lilac grove, which, had it been summer and leafed out, would have blocked my view of anything else beyond it as the moon had already set and blackened the night. The only thing that kept me from thinking the darkness went on forever was a rosy red light that twinkled through the skeletal boundary. It made me think how, just the way winter reduced the grove to knobby features, the boundaries diminished between Betsy and me with time.

It started with Dave and a snow blower, but six or seven years ago when Betsy turned the lilacs over to me, pronounced me grove guardian, we'd made a benchmark. Ever since, Dave and I have mowed all the way around the bush, delineated it from the field on her side of the iron peg; for the past seven years both sides of the sacred boundary have been tended. She even invited Dave to mow a cute little trail to her house through the field that formally disconnected us, violating the authority of the rusty peg. The land showed how we'd been inching closer *spiritually*.

Betsy hadn't really made it into a jar yet; she was the freshest of the bunch, but I wondered how she'd feel about being put into a book instead. Would she approve of my casting? Or of my slant on what had occurred in the pantry? With her concern about appearances, and our history, I knew she'd be interested in how I'd portray her. I expected I might face her again someday and have to account for myself to look. I didn't want looking like a fool who'd only imagined I'd been discerning or helpful to a ghost.

Then I was back in younger skin. In the miracle living room with that young mother in those early morning hours when her child slept in her blood, no more the wiser to it or that life had just taken such a sudden and serious corner. That young mother was there just as certainly as the baby was, just like those women were with me that day on the barren, or Betsy was in my pantry or was now, *standing right beside me sharing the view of the dark night lit by a solitary pinpoint of rosy light.* I'd begun sensing company when, tugged by the little light, my mind wandered out to the lilacs and I was appreciating how thin our boundaries had become. It *seemed* I had evidence of a highly interactive intelligent dimension, spirits standing beside me and a zebra plant, for instance, but then, fools sometimes persist in their folly and memory can make of things what we want.

I refused to satisfy the cursor dramatizing its blank page until I was satisfied I could trust my impressions. My integrity was at stake. So to test the impression that I had a ghost standing beside me, and as she'd been my biggest critic, I asked, *Betsy, do you approve?*

Then, unbelievably to the point, Betsy's exterior lighting sprang on and her stately white house with its wintering landscape declared itself from the January darkness.

It was a glorious way to take my breath away!

I think Betsy was pleased.

It was two-thirty in the morning and no one else was around because they were unconscious, there was just me, the critter that cleverly tripped the motion detector, and the ghosts of Pogey Point.

THE NIGHTMARE
ON BAXTER ROAD
ANATOMY of a
HAUNTING
LEE STRONG

Anatomy of a Haunting

The Nightmare on Baxter Road

LEE STRONG

This is the true story of one couple's descent into darkness. In 1981, Jon and Carlie Summers moved into an inherited home in rural Iowa, leaving behind their workaday lives as a lawyer and a professor in Chicago. Soon after moving in, Jon and Carlie's lives begin a downward spiral as Carlie experiences violent dreams, possessions, hallucinations, and physical illness. Through old journals, nightmares, and personal encounters with evil, Carlie relives the history of the house, embodying its past of abuse, denial, obsession, broken lives, and death.

Anatomy of a Haunting is a terrifying true story that leaves Jon dead and pushes Carlie to the brink of insanity. Through interviews and exhaustive research into the 150-year-old McPherson house, author Lee Strong delves into the history of the haunting and paints a nightmarish picture of one couple's descent into supernatural madness.

978-0-7387-3552-8, 360 pp., 6 x 9 **$16.99**

BARBARA PARKS
in the presence of
spirits
a true story of ghostly visitations

In the Presence of Spirits

A True Story of Ghostly Visitations

BARBARA PARKS

Traumatized by vicious poltergeist attacks that lasted five years, Barbara Parks never imagined that her deep-rooted fear of ghosts would disappear. A momentous turning point occurs when, still mourning the sudden death of a beloved friend, she receives a miraculous visit from him. This joyous experience marks her first step toward healing—and opening up to spirit world.

In the Presence of Spirits chronicles Barbara's uplifting, personal journey of gradually accepting and embracing the clairvoyant gifts that allow her to see spirits. She shares dramatic and heartwarming stories of interacting with spirits who turn up everywhere: at home, on vacation, and accompanying her patients. From the departed uncle that protects Barbara's young children from grave injury to the child spirits who bring comfort to their parents, these amazing true tales are convincing reminders that our loved ones are never far away.

978-0-7387-3352-4, 240 pp., 5³⁄₁₆ x 8 $15.99